Sandeep Ba
March 29
From
63 Alumni

IT'S BACK TO SCHOOL, CHARLIE BROWN!

CHARLES M. SCHULZ

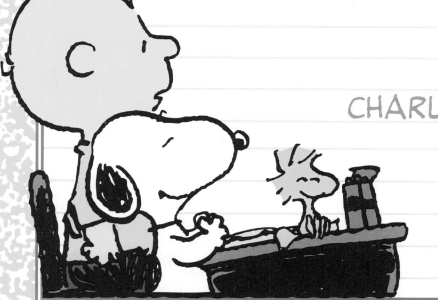

BALLANTINE BOOKS
NEW YORK

A Ballantine Book

Published by The Random House Publishing Group

Copyright © 2003 United Feature Syndicate, Inc.

All rights reserved under International and Pan-American Copyright Conventions. Published in the United States by The Random House

Publishing Group, a division of Random House, Inc., New York, and simultaneously in Canada

by Random House of Canada Limited, Toronto. The comic strips in this book were originally published in newspapers worldwide.

Ballantine and colophon are registered trademarks of Random House, Inc.

www.ballantinebooks.com

A Library of Congress Control Number can be obtained from the publisher upon request.

ISBN 0-345-45283-6

Design by Diane Hobbing of Snap-Haus Graphics

Cover design by United Media

Manufactured in the United States of America

First Edition: August 2003

2   4   6   8   10   9   7   5   3   1

IT'S BACK TO SCHOOL, CHARLIE BROWN!

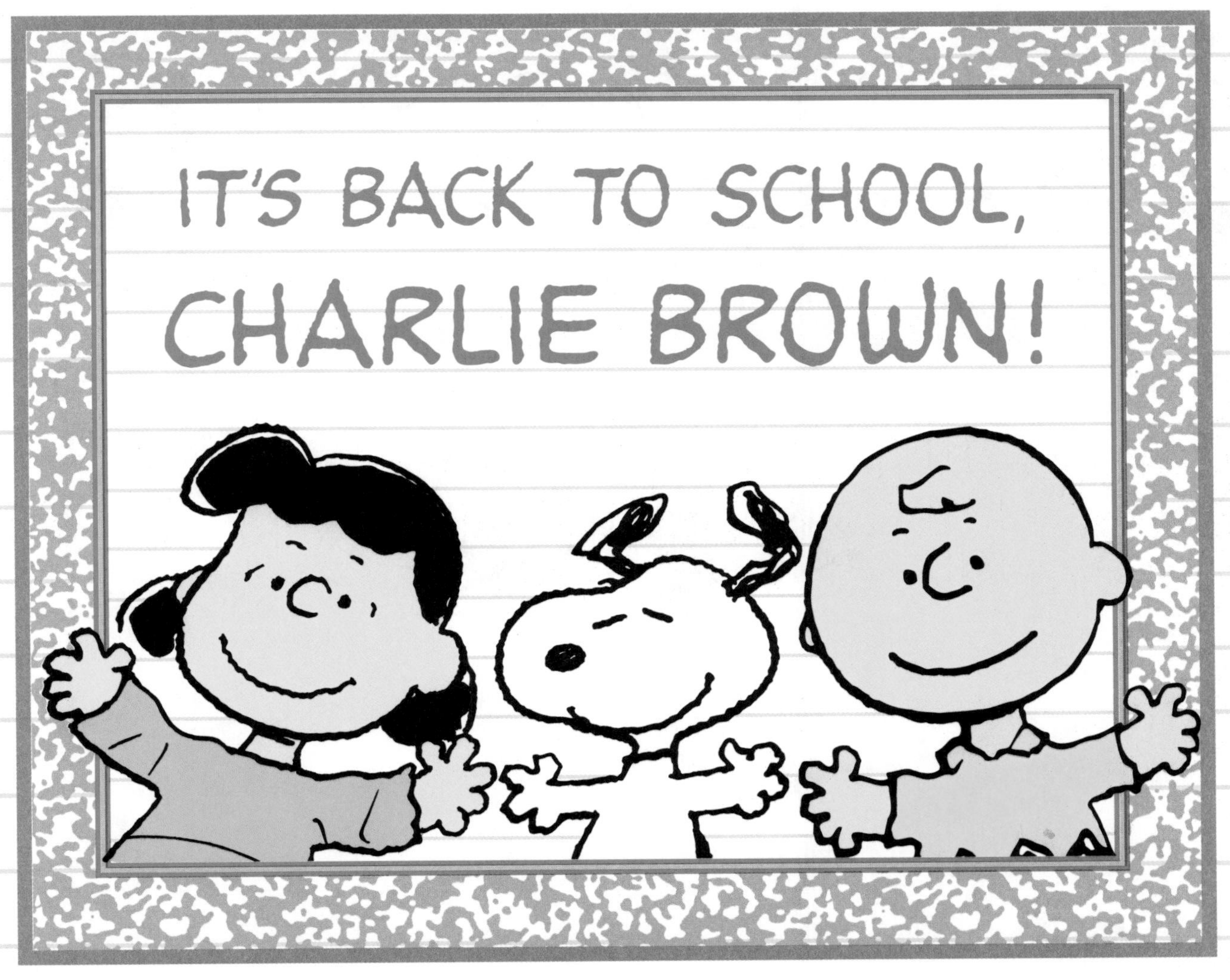

"PEANUTS"
OH, BOY! SCHOOL AGAIN TODAY!!
?
?
HAPPY CAREFREE SCHOOL DAYS
GOOD OL' SCHOOL!
Copr. 1950 by United Feature Syndicate, Inc.
POOR CHARLIE BROWN...HE'S LOST HIS MIND!
11-22
SCHULZ

"PEANUTS"
DOGS HAVE GOT IT EASY
THEY NEVER HAVE TO DO ANYTHING...NOT EVEN GO TO SCHOOL!
YEAH, BUT THEY MISS A LOT, TOO
NO MOVIES, NO BASEBALL, NO TELEVISION...
Copr. 1951 by United Feature Syndicate, Inc
DOGS HAVE REALLY GOT IT ROUGH!
8/10
SCHULZ

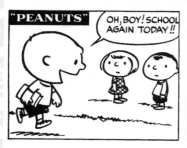

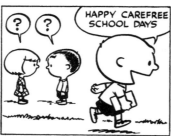

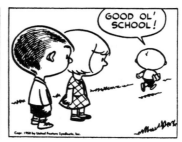

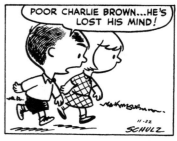

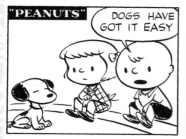

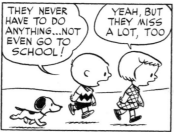

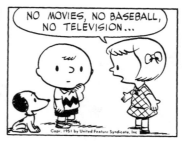

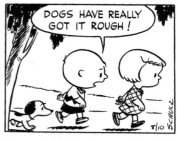

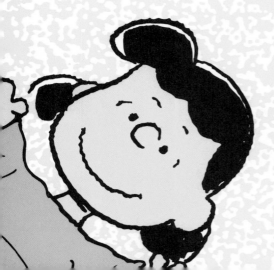

"PEANUTS"
SEPTEMBER IS MY FAVORITE MONTH!
EVERYTHING SEEMS ESPECIALLY BEAUTIFUL IN SEPTEMBER
SCHOOL STARTS THIS MONTH, TOO...
!
I HATE SEPTEMBER!!!
9/10
SCHULZ
Copr. 1951 by United Feature Syndicate, Inc.

"PEANUTS"
GOTTA HURRY! SCHOOL STARTS IN TWO MINUTES!
IT DOES?
RUN! RUN! RUN!
HURRY! HURRY! HURRY!
WHAT AM I RUNNING FOR? I'M TOO YOUNG TO GO TO SCHOOL!
9/18
SCHULZ
Copr. 1951 by United Feature Syndicate, Inc.

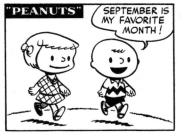

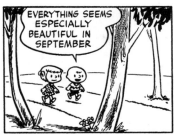

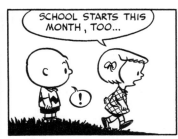

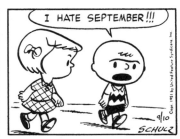

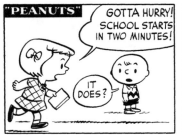

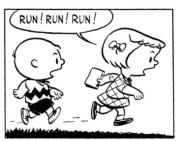

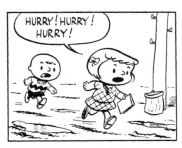

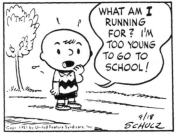

"PEANUTS"
AND THIS IS MY NEW CLOCK...
IT TELLS ME WHEN IT'S TIME TO GET UP, WHEN IT'S TIME TO GO TO SCHOOL AND WHEN IT'S TIME TO GO TO BED...
I DON'T NEED A CLOCK TO TELL ME THAT..
Tm. Reg. U. S. Pat. Off.—All rights reserved Copr. 1952 by United Feature Syndicate, Inc.
MY MOTHER NEVER FORGETS ANY OF THOSE THINGS!
1-28
SCHULZ

"PEANUTS"
HUT, TWO, THREE, FOUR!
HUT, TWO, THREE, FOUR!
HURRY UP, YOU GUYS, OR YOU'LL BE LATE FOR SCHOOL!
THREE MINUS TWO IS HUT!....I MEAN ONE!
Tm. Reg. U. S. Pat. Off.—All rights reserved Copr. 1952 by United Feature Syndicate, Inc.
2-9
SCHULZ

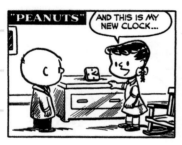

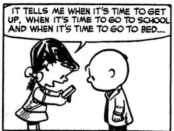

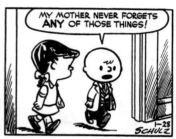

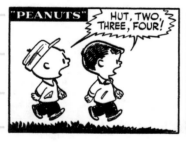

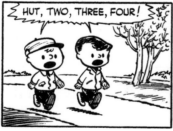

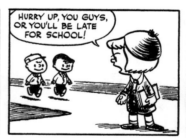

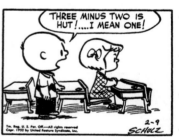

"PEANUTS"
HOW HUMILIATING!
WHAT'S THE MATTER WITH YOU?
I'VE BEEN DISGRACED FOR LIFE!
Tm. Reg. U S Pat Off —All rights reserved Copr 1953 by United Feature Syndicate Inc.
THEY SAY IT'S NEVER HAPPENED TO ANYONE BEFORE
I'VE JUST BEEN EXPELLED FROM NURSERY SCHOOL!
SCHULZ
1-7

"PEANUTS"
I HATE GOING TO SCHOOL
WHY DON'T YOU STAY HOME?
OH, I DON'T FEEL THAT I SHOULD...
OUR TEACHER WORKS SO HARD GETTING THINGS READY EVERY DAY..
I SORT OF FEEL OBLIGATED TO BE THERE!
1-16
SCHULZ

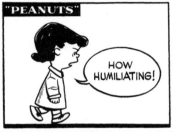

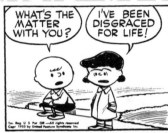

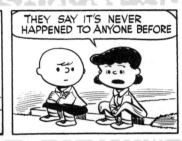

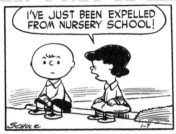

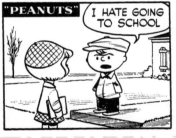

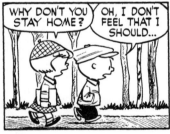

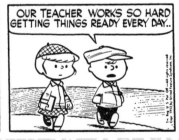

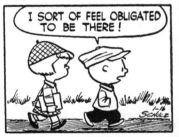

"PEANUTS"
ARE YOU GOING TO NURSERY SCHOOL THESE DAYS, LUCY?
YES, I'VE BEEN REINSTATED
IS IT FUN?
IS IT FUN?! ALL WE HAVE TO DO EVERY DAY IS PLAY PLAY PLAY PLAY PLAY PLAY...
Tm. Reg. U. S. Pat. Off.—All rights reserved Copr. 1953 by United Feature Syndicate, Inc.
I'VE NEVER BEEN SO BORED IN ALL MY LIFE!
1-19
SCHULZ

"PEANUTS"
Tm. Reg. U. S. Pat. Off.—All rights reserved Copr. 1953 by United Feature Syndicate, Inc.
1-29
WHY AREN'T YOU IN SCHOOL?
SCHULZ

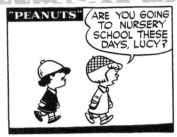

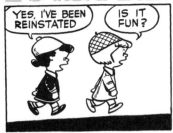

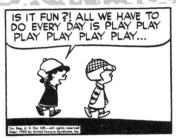

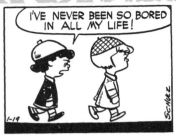

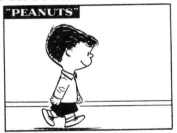

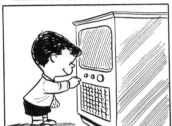

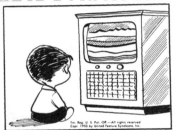

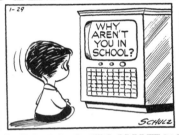

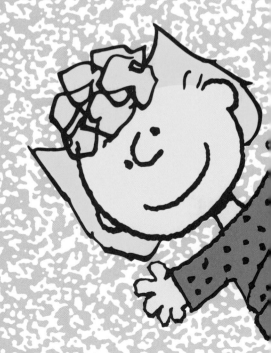

"PEANUTS"
HOW'S NURSERY SCHOOL, LUCY?
O.K., I GUESS....WE DID FINGER-PAINTINGS TODAY
REALLY? THAT'S FUN, ISN'T IT?
I SUPPOSE SO.. MINE DIDN'T TURN OUT VERY WELL..
SCHULZ
I WAS ALL THUMBS
2/23

"PEANUTS"
YOU MEAN YOU'VE QUIT NURSERY SCHOOL ALTOGETHER?
ABSOLUTELY! IT WAS JUST A RACKET!
I WENT THERE FOR OVER SIX WEEKS...TODAY I FOUND OUT IT WAS JUST A RACKET...
THEY DON'T TEACH YOU HOW TO BE A NURSE!
2-28
SCHULZ

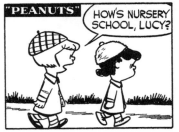

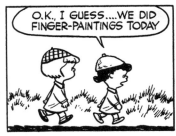

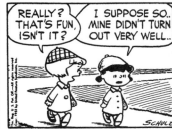

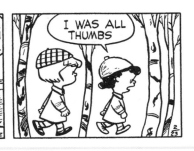

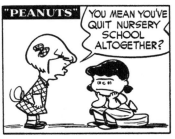

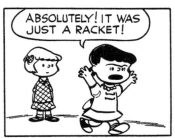

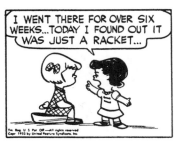

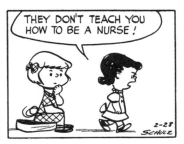

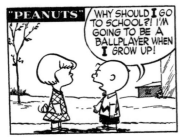

"PEANUTS"
WHY SHOULD I GO TO SCHOOL?! I'M GOING TO BE A BALLPLAYER WHEN I GROW UP!
BALLPLAYERS ONLY HAVE TO BE ABLE TO COUNT BALLS AND STRIKES!
OH, YEAH? THINK AGAIN, CHARLIE BROWN..
YOU WON'T EVEN BE ABLE TO TELL IF YOU'VE GOT ENOUGH PLAYERS ON THE FIELD...YOU WON'T BE ABLE TO COUNT THAT HIGH!
!
YOU'RE RIGHT... I'D BETTER GO UNTIL I LEARN TO COUNT TO NINE..
10-8
SCHULZ

"PEANUTS"
I'VE COME TO A CONCLUSION...
I THINK MY FOLKS ARE SENDING ME TO NURSERY SCHOOL JUST TO GET ME OUT OF THE HOUSE!
THEY PAID I DON'T KNOW HOW MUCH FOR ME IN THE FIRST PLACE,..
AND NOW THEY PAY FIVE DOLLARS A WEEK JUST TO GET RID OF ME!
10-10
SCHULZ

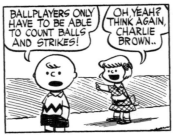

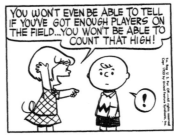

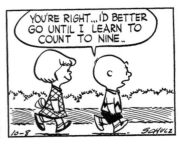

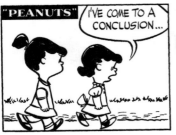

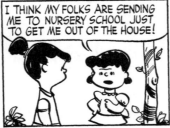

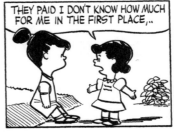

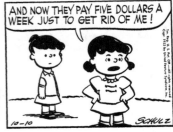

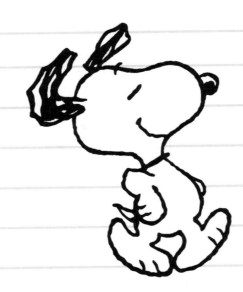

"PEANUTS"
HURRY! HURRY!
I CAN'T RUN ANY FASTER!
?
SCHOOL STARTS IN THREE MINUTES!
WE'LL NEVER MAKE IT!
ONCE IN A WHILE IT'S KIND OF NICE BEING JUST A DOG..
SCHULZ
Tm. Reg. U. S. Pat. Off.—All rights reserved
Copr. 1953 by United Feature Syndicate, Inc.
10-26

"PEANUTS"
I'M THROUGH WITH SCHOOL! I QUIT!
QUIT?! HA! YOU MUST BE CRAZY, CHARLIE BROWN!
YOU CAN'T QUIT SCHOOL! THEY WON'T LET YOU! YOU'VE GOT TO GO FOR TWELVE MORE YEARS!
DID YOU HEAR ME? TWELVE MORE YEARS! TWELVE LONG YEARS! EVERY DAY! YEAR IN AND YEAR OUT! TWELVE YEARS! TWELVE..
Tm. Reg. U. S. Pat. Off.—All rights reserved
Copr. 1953 by United Feature Syndicate, Inc.
YAAH!
11-13
SCHULZ

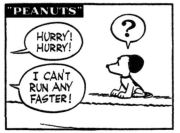

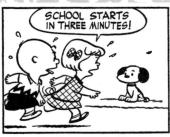

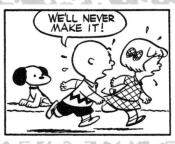

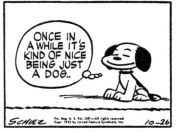

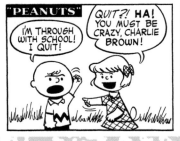

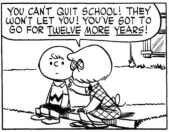

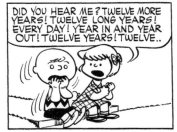

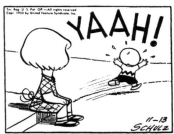

"PEANUTS"
YOU KNOW WHAT?
WHAT?
MY GRANDFATHER SAYS WHEN HE WENT TO SCHOOL, HE USED TO DUNK THE GIRLS' PIGTAILS IN THE INKWELL..
MY GRANDFATHER SAYS WHEN HE WENT TO SCHOOL, HE USED TO DUNK THE GIRLS' PIGTAILS IN THE INKWELL..
IF YOU TRY THAT, I'LL KNOCK YOU CLEAR ACROSS TH' ROOM

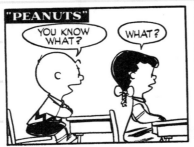

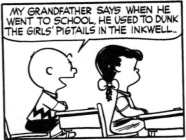

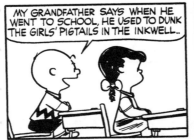

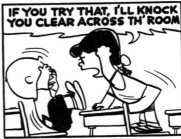

"PEANUTS"
THAT DID IT! I'M NEVER GOING TO SCHOOL AGAIN!
WHAT A GYP! I WROTE THIS TERRIFIC STORY FOR ENGLISH, SEE? TODAY THE TEACHER HANDS IT BACK
YOU KNOW WHAT I GOT FOR IT?! 'VERY GOOD'!
WHAT DID YOU EXPECT?
MONEY!
3-21
SCHULZ

"PEANUTS"
I GUESS IT'S JUST NO USE..
EVERYTHING I LEARN I LEARN THE HARD WAY!
WHAT WAY IS THAT, CHARLIE BROWN?
IN SCHOOL!
SCHULZ
8-27

"PEANUTS"
HOW'S KINDERGARTEN, LUCY?
GOOD ENOUGH, I GUESS, CONSIDERING IT REALLY ISN'T WHAT I HAD WANTED..
OH? HAD YOU WANTED TO GO SOMEPLACE ELSE?
SURE..
MILITARY SCHOOL!
9-20
SCHULZ

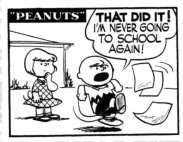

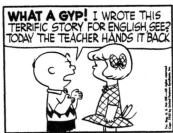

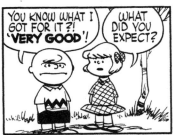

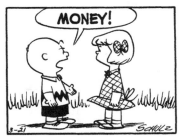

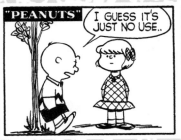

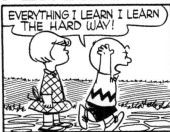

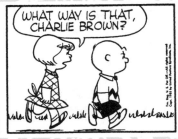

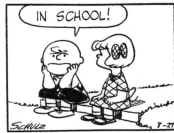

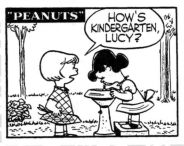

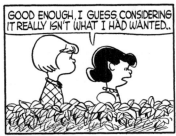

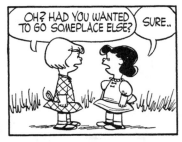

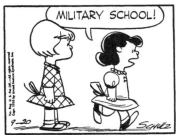

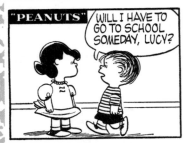

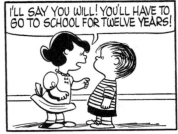

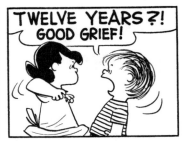

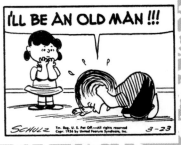

"PEANUTS"
WILL I HAVE TO GO TO SCHOOL SOMEDAY, LUCY?
I'LL SAY YOU WILL! YOU'LL HAVE TO GO TO SCHOOL FOR TWELVE YEARS!
TWELVE YEARS?! GOOD GRIEF!
I'LL BE AN OLD MAN!!!
SCHULZ
Tm. Reg. U. S. Pat. Off.—All rights reserved Copr. 1956 by United Feature Syndicate, Inc.
3-23

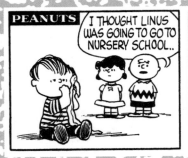

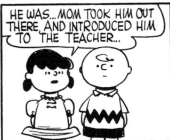

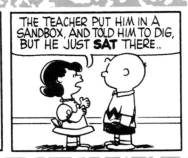

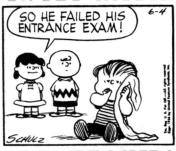

PEANUTS
I THOUGHT LINUS WAS GOING TO GO TO NURSERY SCHOOL..
HE WAS...MOM TOOK HIM OUT THERE, AND INTRODUCED HIM TO THE TEACHER...
THE TEACHER PUT HIM IN A SANDBOX, AND TOLD HIM TO DIG, BUT HE JUST SAT THERE..
SO HE FAILED HIS ENTRANCE EXAM!
6-4
SCHULZ

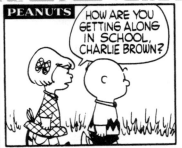

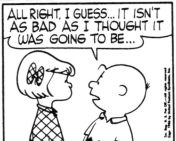

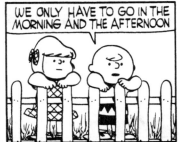

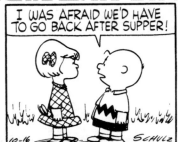

PEANUTS
HOW ARE YOU GETTING ALONG IN SCHOOL, CHARLIE BROWN?
ALL RIGHT, I GUESS... IT ISN'T AS BAD AS I THOUGHT IT WAS GOING TO BE...
WE ONLY HAVE TO GO IN THE MORNING AND THE AFTERNOON
I WAS AFRAID WE'D HAVE TO GO BACK AFTER SUPPER!
10-16
SCHULZ

"PEANUTS"
CHARLIE BROWN, DID YOU KNOW THAT TWELVE-THOUSAND HOURS OF YOUR LIFE WILL BE SPENT IN SCHOOL?
REALLY? WHY, THAT'S INCREDIBLE!
IT'S FANTASTIC...IT'S UNBELIEVABLE...
IT'S ALSO ENOUGH TO MAKE YOU SICK...
10-24
SCHULZ

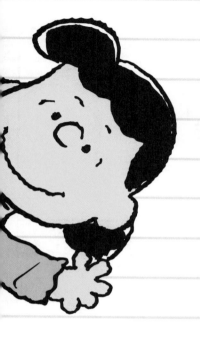

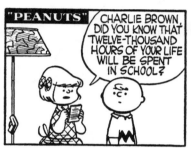

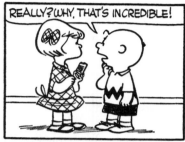

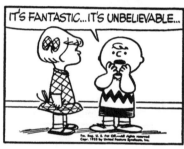

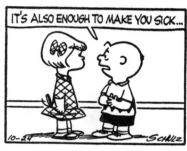

PEANUTS
HOW'S NURSERY SCHOOL COMING, LINUS?
OKAY, I GUESS...THE TEACHER SPENDS THE FIRST HOUR HELPING EVERYBODY OFF WITH THEIR HATS AND COATS AND EVERYTHING..
Tm. Reg. U. S. Pat. Off.—All rights reserved
Copr. 1957 by United Feature Syndicate, Inc.
THEN WHAT?
THEN IT'S TIME TO PUT 'EM ALL BACK ON, AND GO HOME!
9-27
SCHULZ

PEANUTS
HOW'S NURSERY SCHOOL COMING ALONG, LINUS?
OKAY, I GUESS
BUT I HAVE THE FEELING MY MOTHER IS SENDING ME JUST TO GET ME OUT OF THE HOUSE FOR A FEW HOURS..
10-1
THAT'S A DEPRESSING THOUGHT, ISN'T IT?
Tm. Reg. U. S. Pat. Off.—All rights reserved
Copr. 1957 by United Feature Syndicate, Inc.
SCHULZ

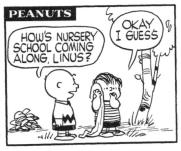

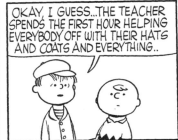

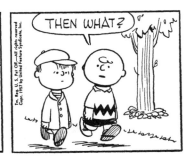

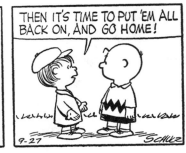

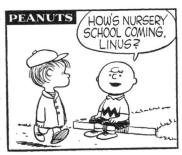

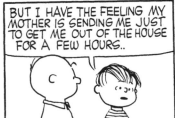

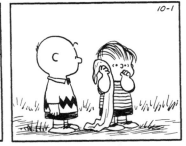

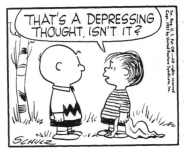

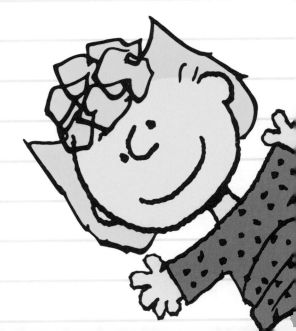

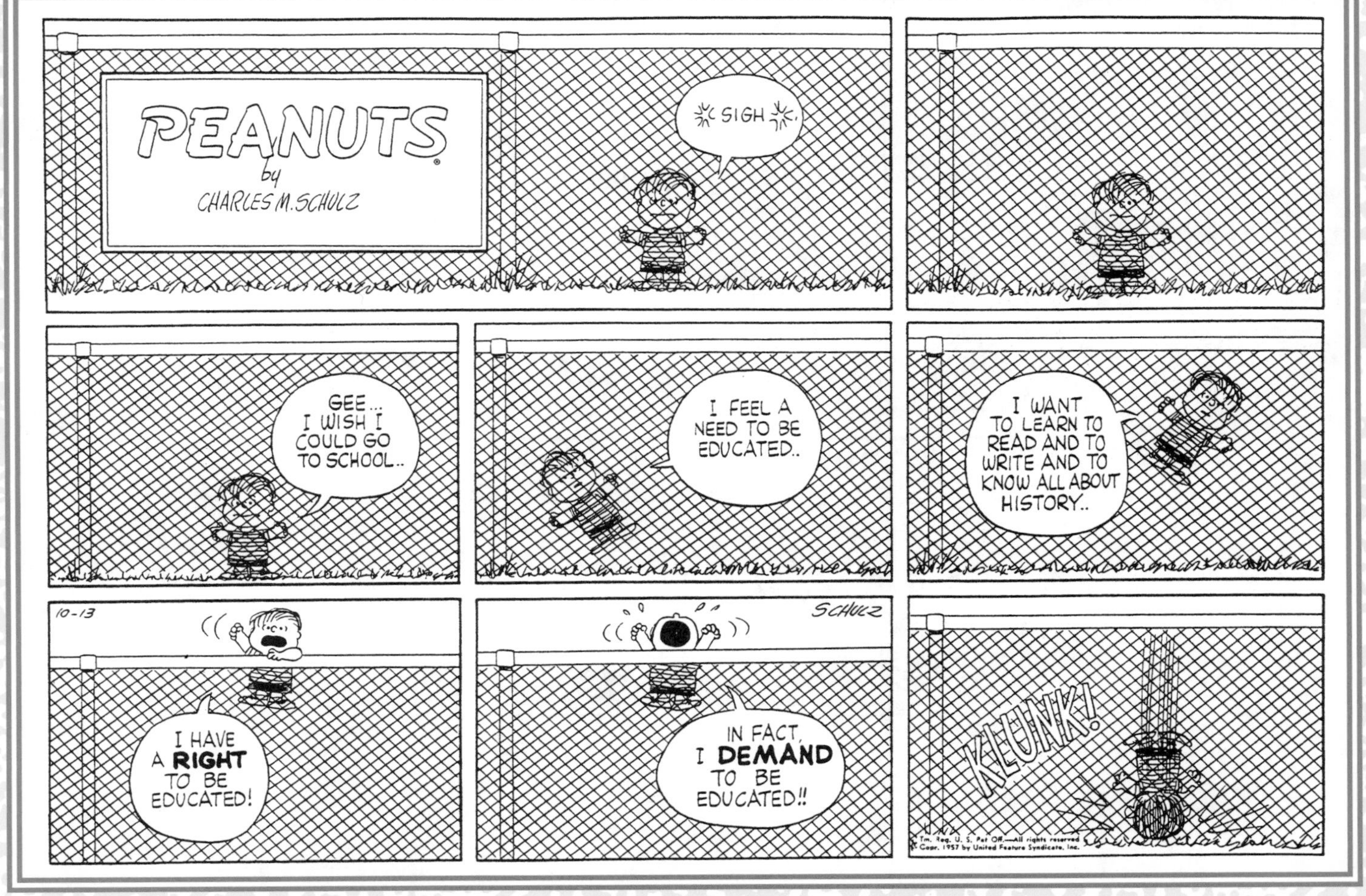
PEANUTS
by
CHARLES M. SCHULZ
SIGH
GEE... I WISH I COULD GO TO SCHOOL..
I FEEL A NEED TO BE EDUCATED..
I WANT TO LEARN TO READ AND TO WRITE AND TO KNOW ALL ABOUT HISTORY..
10-13
I HAVE A **RIGHT** TO BE EDUCATED!
SCHULZ
IN FACT, I **DEMAND** TO BE EDUCATED!!
KLUNK!
Tm. Reg. U. S. Pat. Off.—All rights reserved
© Copr. 1957 by United Feature Syndicate, Inc.

PEANUTS
Tm. Reg. U. S. Pat Off.—All rights reserved
Copr. 1957 by United Feature Syndicate, Inc.
WELL! THERE HE IS!
MY PAL!!
11-14
EVERYONE SHOULD HAVE A DOG TO GREET HIM WHEN HE COMES HOME!
SCHULZ

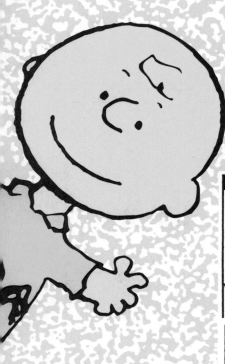

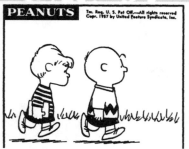

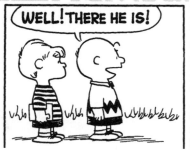

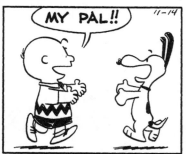

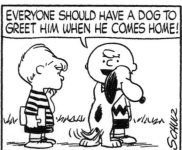

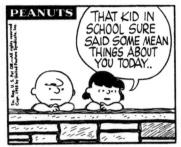

PEANUTS
THAT KID IN SCHOOL SURE SAID SOME MEAN THINGS ABOUT YOU TODAY..
HOW COME YOU DIDN'T HIT HIM?
I HAVE OBSERVED THAT WHENEVER YOU TRY TO HIT SOMEBODY, THERE IS A TENDENCY FOR THEM TO TRY TO HIT YOU BACK
YOU ARE A SHREWD JUDGE OF HUMAN NATURE, CHARLIE BROWN
SCHULZ
5-6

PEANUTS
SCHOOL IS GETTING YOU DOWN, ISN'T IT, CHARLIE BROWN?
WHEN YOU COME HOME IN THE AFTERNOON, YOU NEED SOMETHING TO HELP YOU TO UNWIND...YOU NEED TO RELAX..
I KNOW I DO...
BUT WHO WANTS TO LIE WITH HIS HEAD IN A WATER DISH?!
SCHULZ
5-8

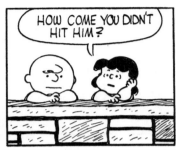

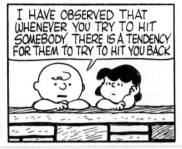

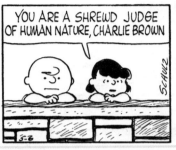

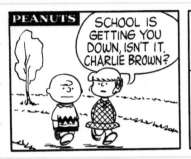

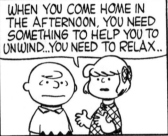

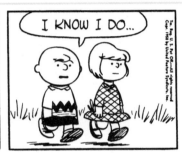

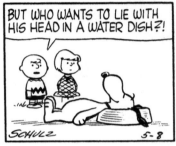

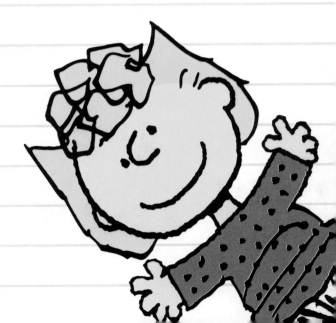

PEANUTS
DEAR PENCIL-PAL, HOW DO YOU GO TO SCHOOL? I RIDE IN A SCHOOL BUS.
I GO TO A BIG SCHOOL. WE LEARN A LOT IN OUR SCHOOL.
THEY TEACH US SCIENCE, ENGLISH, GEOGRAPHY, ARITHAMETIC, HISTORY AND SPELLING.
9-3
WHEN I GET BIG I WOULD LIKE TO DRIVE A SCHOOL BUS.
Tm. Reg. U. S. Pat. Off.—All rights reserved
Copr. 1958 by United Feature Syndicate, Inc.
SCHULZ

PEANUTS
KINDERGARTEN IS AS FAR AS I'M GOING TO GO!
AS SOON AS I'M THROUGH WITH KINDERGARTEN, I'M GOING TO DROP OUT OF SCHOOL!
Tm. Reg. U. S. Pat. Off.—All rights reserved
Copr. 1958 by United Feature Syndicate, Inc.
10-6
AS FAR AS I'M CONCERNED, THAT'S IT!
THERE'S NOTHING THAT CAN HARM A PERSON MORE THAN TOO MUCH FORMAL EDUCATION!
SCHULZ

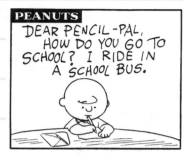

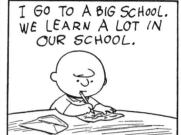

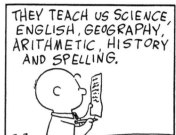

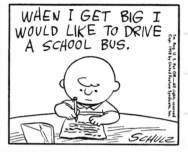

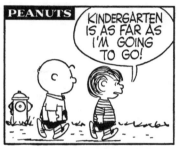

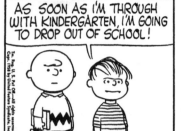

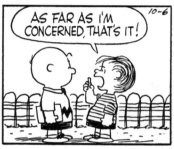

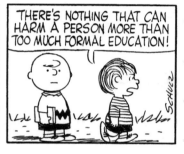

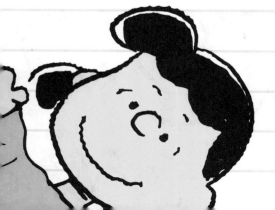

PEANUTS
AFTER KINDERGARTEN YOU GO TO SCHOOL FOR TWELVE MORE YEARS...
THEN YOU GO TO COLLEGE FOR MAYBE FOUR OR SIX OR EIGHT MORE YEARS..
THEN WHAT?
THEN YOU CAN DO ANYTHING YOU WANT TO..
Tm. Reg. U. S. Pat. Off.—All rights reserved
Copr. 1958 by United Feature Syndicate, Inc.
10-7
HOW NICE OF THEM!
SCHULZ

PEANUTS
Tm. Reg. U. S. Pat. Off.—All rights reserved
Copr. 1958 by United Feature Syndicate, Inc.
"KINDERGARTEN.." LET'S SEE...
"A SCHOOL OR CLASS FOR YOUNG CHILDREN THAT DEVELOPS BASIC SKILLS AND SOCIAL BEHAVIOR BY GAMES, EXERCISES...
..AND SIMPLE HANDICRAFT."
10-9
SCHULZ

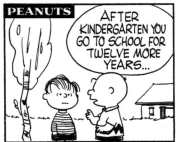

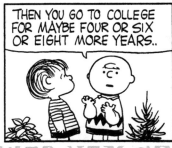

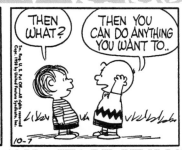

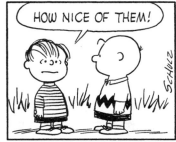

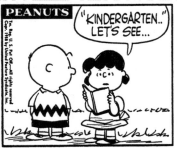

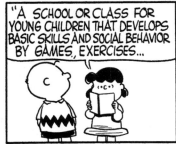

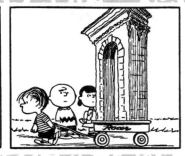

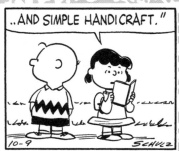

PEANUTS
DEAR?PENCIL-PAL?
HOW?ARE? YOU?
DOING?IN?SCHOOL?
WE?LEARN?
SOMETHING?NEW?
EVERY? DAY?
10-16
TODAY?WE?LEARNED?
HOW?TO?MAKE?
QUESTION?MARKS?
SCHULZ

PEANUTS
I FOUND A NEW FRIEND AT SCHOOL
HE'S JUST ABOUT MY SIZE..
10-30
AND POLITE...HE'S SO POLITE..
YOU CAN HIT HIM, AND HE DOESN'T HIT YOU BACK!
SCHULZ

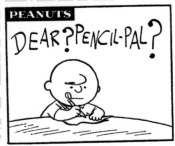

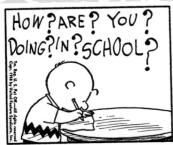

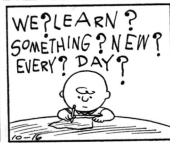

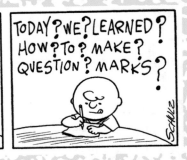

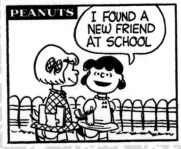

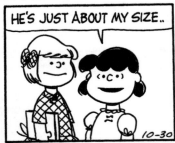

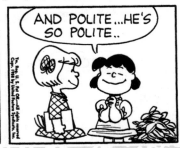

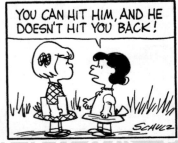

PEANUTS
SOME STARS ARE BIG, AND SOME STARS ARE LITTLE
YOU SURE KNOW A LOT ABOUT THE STARS, LUCY..
Tm. Reg. U. S. Pat. Off.—All rights reserved Copr. 1959 by United Feature Syndicate, Inc.
WELL, I'VE DONE QUITE A BIT OF STUDYING...
ONE OF MY BEST SUBJECTS IN SCHOOL WAS AGRICULTURE!
1-27
SCHULZ

PEANUTS
HOW ARE YOU DOING IN SCHOOL THESE DAYS, CHARLIE BROWN?
OH, FAIRLY WELL, I GUESS... I'M HAVING MOST OF MY TROUBLE IN ARITHMETIC..
Tm. Reg. U. S. Pat. Off.—All rights reserved Copr. 1959 by United Feature Syndicate, Inc.
I SHOULD THINK YOU'D LIKE ARITHMETIC...IT'S A VERY PRECISE SUBJECT..
2-25
THAT'S JUST THE TROUBLE.. I'M AT MY BEST IN SOMETHING WHERE THE ANSWERS ARE MOSTLY A MATTER OF OPINION!
SCHULZ

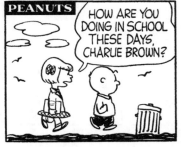

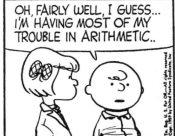

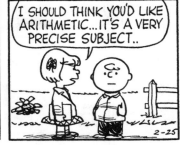

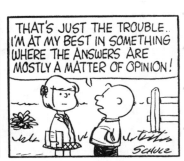

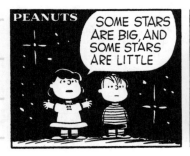

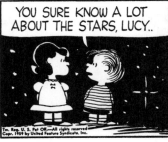

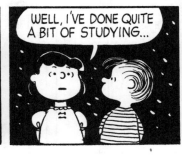

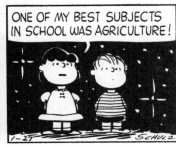

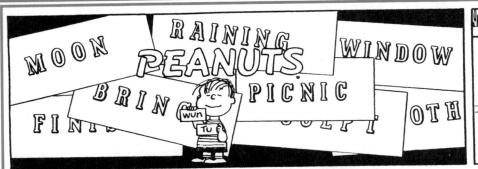

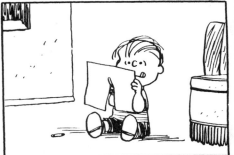

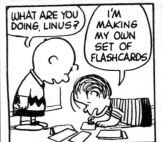

MOON
RAINING
WINDOW
PEANUTS
BRING
PICNIC
WUN
TU
OTH
WHAT ARE YOU DOING, LINUS?
I'M MAKING MY OWN SET OF FLASHCARDS
THESE ARE JUST LIKE THE ONES THEY USE IN SCHOOL, AND THEY'RE A GREAT AID IN LEARNING TO READ..
LOOOK
I'LL HOLD THEM UP, CHARLIE BROWN, AND WE'LL SEE HOW GOOD A READER YOU ARE...
READY?
LOOOK
UH HUH!
VERY GOOD...NOW TRY THE NEXT ONE..
7-19
TAYBUL
GOOD.. AND THE NEXT?
KOW
VERY GOOD.. NOW LET'S GO A LITTLE FASTER..
PAYPUR, DORE, HOWSE, WELKUM, NIFE, SPUNE!
EXCELLENT! DO YOU WANT TO RUN THROUGH THEM AGAIN?
NO, I THINK ONCE IS ENOUGH...
AWL THYS REEDING IS HARRD ONN MI EYYS!
SCHULZ

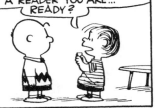

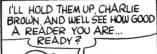

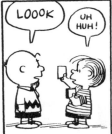

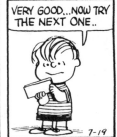

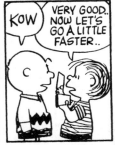

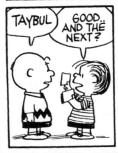

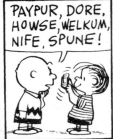

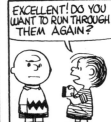

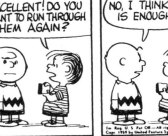

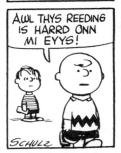

PEANUTS
HERE'S THE FAITHFUL DOG FOLLOWING THE KIDS TO SCHOOL..
HERE'S THE FAITHFUL DOG SITTING DOWN OUTSIDE WHILE ALL THE KIDS GO INSIDE..
HERE'S THE FAITHFUL DOG LYING DOWN OUTSIDE WAITING FOR SCHOOL TO LET OUT...
10-12
Tm. Reg. U. S. Pat Off.—All rights reserved Copr. 1959 by United Feature Syndicate, Inc.
HERE'S THE FAITHFUL DOG SUDDENLY REALIZING HE'S WASTING HIS TIME!
SCHULZ

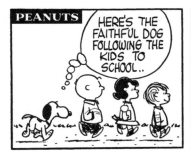

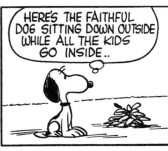

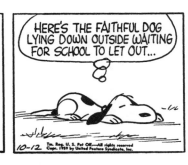

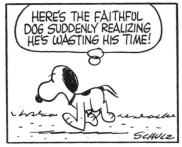

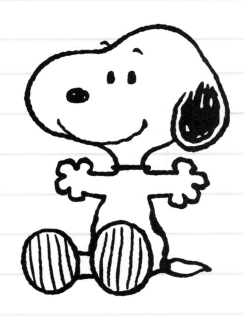

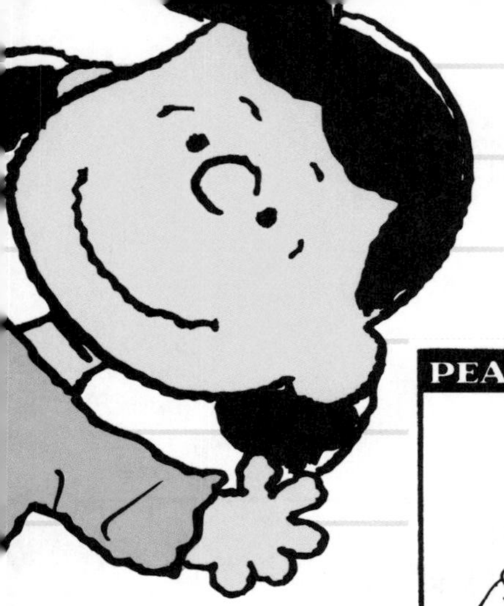

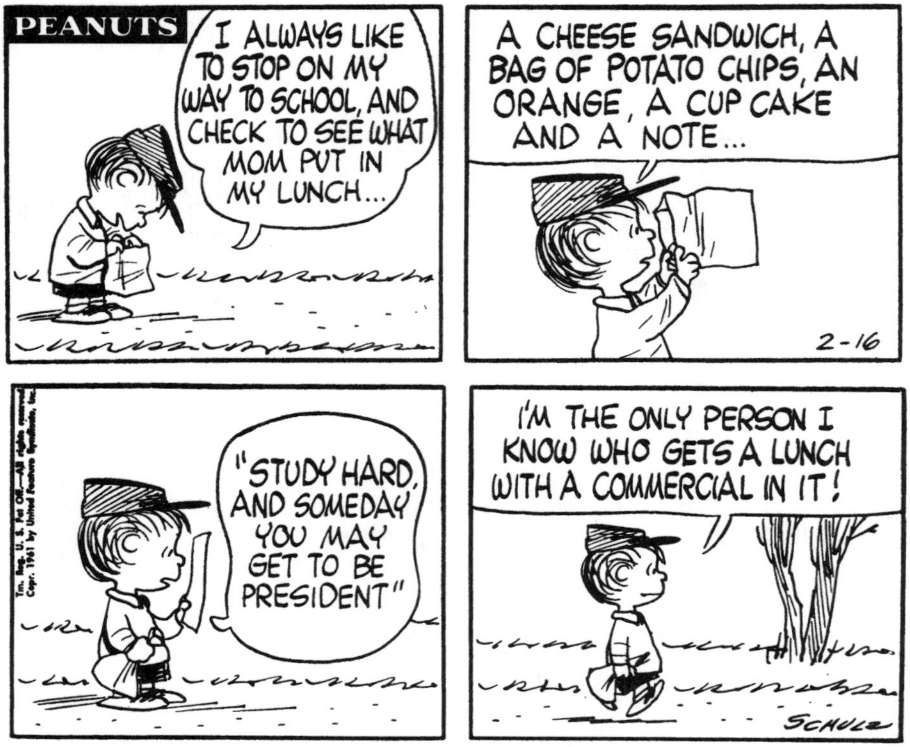
PEANUTS
I ALWAYS LIKE TO STOP ON MY WAY TO SCHOOL, AND CHECK TO SEE WHAT MOM PUT IN MY LUNCH...
A CHEESE SANDWICH, A BAG OF POTATO CHIPS, AN ORANGE, A CUP CAKE AND A NOTE...
2-16
Tm. Reg. U. S. Pat. Off.—All rights reserved
Copr. 1961 by United Feature Syndicate, Inc.
"STUDY HARD, AND SOMEDAY YOU MAY GET TO BE PRESIDENT"
I'M THE ONLY PERSON I KNOW WHO GETS A LUNCH WITH A COMMERCIAL IN IT!
SCHULZ

PEANUTS
I ALWAYS ENJOY READING THE LITTLE NOTES MY MOTHER PUTS IN MY LUNCH..
2-22
HMM...SO NOW SHE'S A COMEDIENNE...
Tm. Reg. U. S. Pat. Off.—All rights reserved
Copr. 1961 by United Feature Syndicate, Inc.
WHY? WHAT DOES SHE SAY?
"HELP! I'M BEING HELD PRISONER IN A SCHOOL LUNCH FACTORY!"
SCHULZ

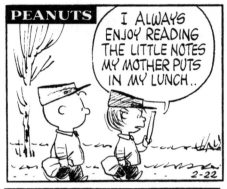

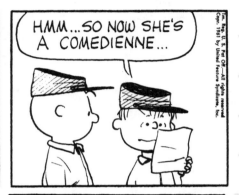

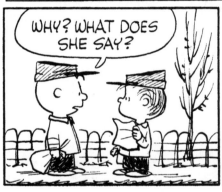

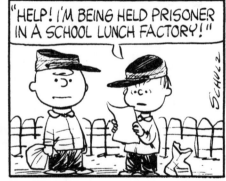

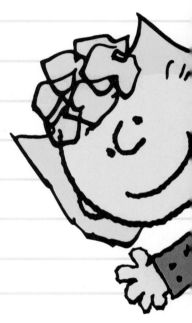

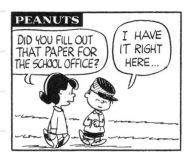

PEANUTS
DID YOU FILL OUT THAT PAPER FOR THE SCHOOL OFFICE?
I HAVE IT RIGHT HERE...
MY MOTHER'S NAME, MY FATHER'S NAME, OUR ADDRESS AND OUR TELEPHONE NUMBER...
Tm. Reg. U. S. Pat. Off.—All rights reserved Copr. 1961 by United Feature Syndicate, Inc.
4-21
WHAT DID YOU PUT DOWN UNDER "FAMILY PHYSICIAN"?
WELL, I WASN'T SURE SO I PUT DOWN "DR. SEUSS"!
SCHULZ

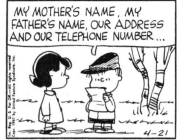

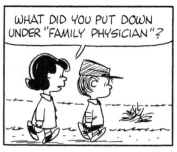

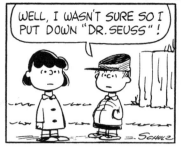

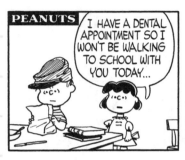

PEANUTS
I HAVE A DENTAL APPOINTMENT SO I WON'T BE WALKING TO SCHOOL WITH YOU TODAY...
I'LL SEE YOU WHEN YOU GET HOME...
OKAY
HAVE A GOOD DAY AT SCHOOL...
Tm. Reg. U. S. Pat. Off.—All rights reserved Copr. 1961 by United Feature Syndicate, Inc.
5-29
LEARN THINGS!
SCHULZ

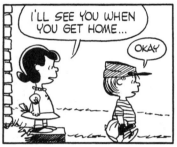

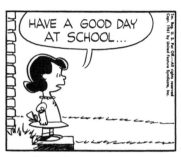

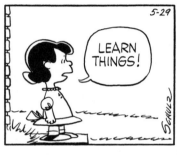

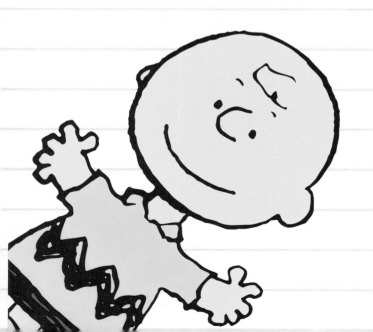

PEANUTS
IT WAS GOOD TO BE BACK IN SCHOOL AGAIN...
IT WAS GOOD JUST TO SIT THERE AND WATCH MISS OTHMAR IN ACTION...
Tm. Reg. U. S. Pat Off.—All rights reserved Copr. 1961 by United Feature Syndicate, Inc.
OF COURSE, I ADMIRE **ALL** TEACHERS, BUT MISS OTHMAR IS A GEM AMONG GEMS...
9-7
ONE WONDERS WHAT THE NATIONAL EDUCATION ASSOCIATION DID TO DESERVE SUCH A BREAK
SCHULZ

PEANUTS
THERE GO ALL THE KIDS... OFF TO SCHOOL!
I WISH WE COULD GO TO SCHOOL, SNOOPY...
BUT THEY WON'T LET YOU GO TO SCHOOL UNTIL YOU'RE FIVE YEARS OLD...
Tm. Reg. U. S. Pat Off.—All rights reserved Copr. 1961 by United Feature Syndicate, Inc.
..AND CAN PROVE THAT YOU'RE A HUMAN BEING!
10-16
SCHULZ

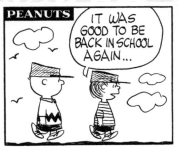

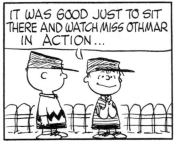

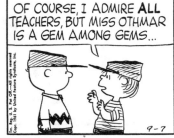

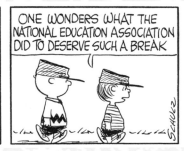

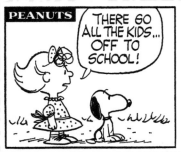

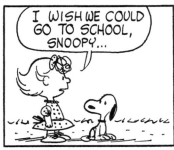

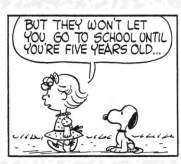

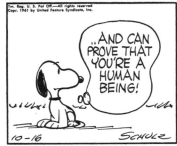

PEANUTS
Tm. Reg. U. S. Pat. Off.—All rights reserved
Copr. 1960 by United Feature Syndicate, Inc.
WHEN YOU'RE ON YOUR WAY TO SCHOOL, AND YOU MEET A DOG, YOU SHOULD ALWAYS STOP, AND PAT HIM ON THE HEAD...
PAT PAT
THAT ALWAYS GETS YOUR DAY OFF TO A GOOD START..
SCHULZ 12-27
WELL, AT LEAST I'M CONTRIBUTING **SOMETHING** TO SOCIETY!

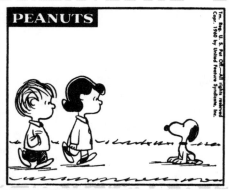

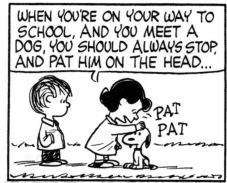

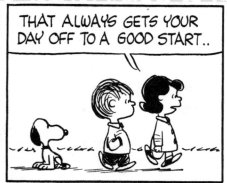

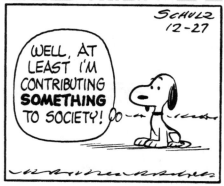

PEANUTS
WELL, SALLY, IN A COUPLE MORE WEEKS YOU'LL BE STARTING KINDERGARTEN
KINDERGARTEN?
8-20
SURE... EVERYBODY HAS TO GO TO SCHOOL..
SCHOOL?!
OF COURSE! THIS IS THE WAY YOU BECOME EDUCATED..
EDUCATED?
Tm. Reg. U. S. Pat. Off.—All rights reserved Copr. 1962 by United Feature Syndicate, Inc.
I SEE TROUBLE AHEAD FOR SOME POOR TEACHER..
TEACHER?
SCHULZ

PEANUTS
Tm. Reg. U. S. Pat. Off.—All rights reserved Copr. 1962 by United Feature Syndicate, Inc.
ISN'T THERE ANY WAY I CAN GET OUT OF STARTING KINDERGARTEN?
8-21
I DOUBT IT, SALLY...EVERYBODY HAS TO GO SCHOOL...
THERE **MUST** BE SOME WAY OF GETTING AROUND IT...
DO YOU THINK MAYBE I COULD GET A DEFERMENT?
SCHULZ

PEANUTS
Tm. Reg. U. S. Pat. Off.—All rights reserved Copr. 1962 by United Feature Syndicate, Inc.
ACTUALLY, I'M SORT OF AFRAID TO GO TO SCHOOL..
I HEAR THEY ASK YOU A LOT OF QUESTIONS...IS THIS TRUE?
YES, I GUESS SO...WHY SHOULD THIS BOTHER YOU?
THERE ARE CERTAIN THINGS I'D JUST RATHER NOT HAVE BROUGHT UP!
8-23
SCHULZ

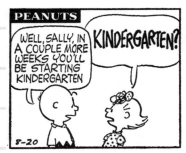

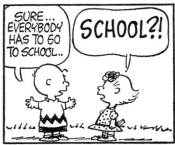

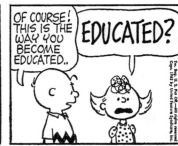

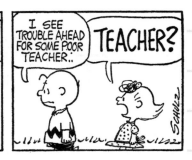

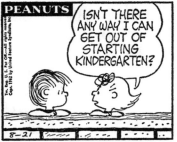

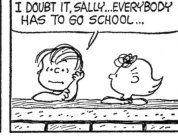

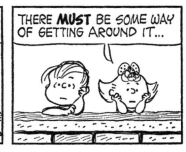

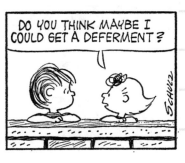

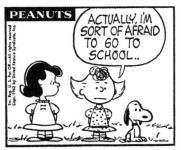

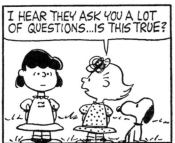

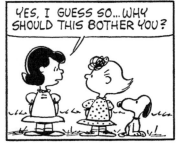

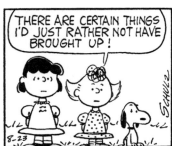

PEANUTS
Tm. Reg. U. S. Pat. Off.—All rights reserved
Copr. 1962 by United Feature Syndicate, Inc.
LOOK, SALLY, YOU'RE GOING TO HAVE TO GO TO SCHOOL SO YOU MIGHT AS WELL GET USED TO THE IDEA!
8-24
I GUESS YOU'RE RIGHT...I'LL JUST HAVE TO MAKE THE BEST OF IT..
I'LL GO TO KINDERGARTEN, AND I'LL STUDY, AND I'LL PLAY ALL THEIR GAMES, AND I'LL TRY TO GET ALONG WITH EVERYBODY...
BUT I WON'T LEARN LATIN!!
SCHULZ

PEANUTS
Tm. Reg. U. S. Pat. Off.—All rights reserved
Copr. 1962 by United Feature Syndicate, Inc.
I'M NOT THE GOING-TO-SCHOOL TYPE!
I CAN'T REMEMBER WHERE THE LONGEST RIVER IS OR HOW HIGH ALL THOSE MOUNTAINS ARE! I CAN'T REMEMBER ALL THOSE ENGLISH KINGS!
I CAN'T REMEMBER ALL THAT STUFF ABOUT THE LEGISLATIVE BRANCH AND THE STATES AND THE ELECTRICAL VOTES AND WHO THE VICE-PRESIDENT WAS AND ALL THAT! I CAN'T!
8-29
I DON'T WANT TO GO TO KINDERGARTEN!
SCHULZ

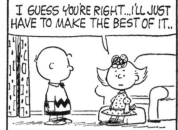

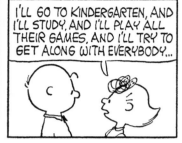

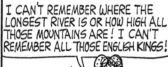

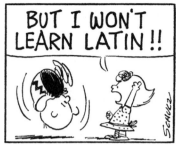

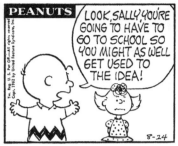

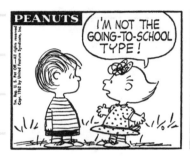

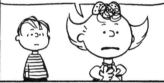

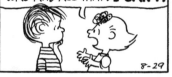

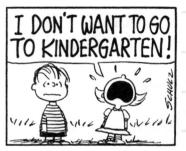

PEANUTS

I THINK YOUR SISTER NEEDS HELP, CHARLIE BROWN...

THIS FEAR SHE HAS OF STARTING KINDERGARTEN IS BEYOND THE NORMAL FEARS OF PRE-SCHOOL CHILDREN.. I REALLY THINK SHE NEEDS PROFESSIONAL HELP...

8-30

PERHAPS YOU'RE RIGHT..

PSYCHIATRIC CARE 5¢

THE DOCTOR IS **IN**

SCHULZ

PEANUTS

TOMORROW IS THE FIRST DAY OF SCHOOL..

POOR SALLY IS SO NERVOUS THAT IF SOMEONE MENTIONED KINDERGARTEN, I BET SHE'D JUMP THIRTY FEET IN THE AIR..

9-4

KINDERGARTEN!

ONLY TEN FEET... I KNEW YOU WERE EXAGGERATING..

PEANUTS WELL, SALLY, TODAY'S THE FIRST DAY OF SCHOOL...

WE'LL SOON BE THERE....JUST A LITTLE WAY TO GO NOW...

THERE IT IS...THERE'S YOUR SCHOOL...

AAUGH!

9-5

PEANUTS I HEAR YOU'RE HAVING TROUBLE WITH READING IN SCHOOL, CHARLIE BROWN..

YES, I'VE BEEN WONDERING IF I NEED GLASSES..

I DOUBT IT..

9-13

MY OPHTHALMOLOGIST SAID THAT THE CAUSE OF SLOW READING IS SELDOM OCULAR... YOU PROBABLY HAVE "MIXED BRAIN DOMINANCE"

THAT'S THE NICEST THING ANYONE HAS EVER SAID TO ME!

PEANUTS
ANOTHER NOTE FROM YOUR MOTHER?
YES, SHE LIKES TO PUT THEM IN WITH MY LUNCH
10-12
"DEAR SON, ARE YOU STUDYING HARD TODAY? HAVE YOU MADE THE MOST OF THE MORNING HOURS?
Tm. Reg. U. S. Pat. Off.—All rights reserved Copr. 1962 by United Feature Syndicate, Inc.
YOUR FATHER AND I WANT ONLY THE BEST FOR YOU, BUT YOU MUST DO YOUR PART, TOO....DON'T FAIL US...BE DILIGENT...LOVINGLY, MOM"
I USED TO WONDER WHY YOU SOMETIMES DRAG THAT BLANKET AROUND, BUT NOW I THINK I KNOW!
SCHULZ

PEANUTS
TELL MOM I DON'T THINK I'LL GO TO SCHOOL TODAY..TELL HER I'M EMOTIONALLY EXHAUSTED...
SHE SAYS TO GET OUT OF BED THIS VERY MINUTE!
12-17
Tm. Reg. U. S. Pat. Off.—All rights reserved Copr. 1962 by United Feature Syndicate, Inc.
NICE TRY!
SCHULZ

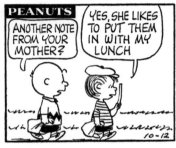

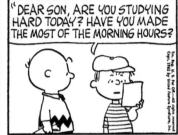

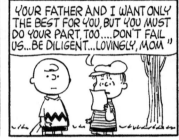

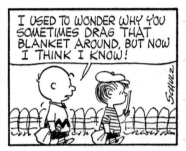

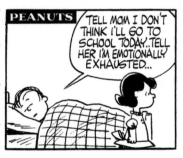

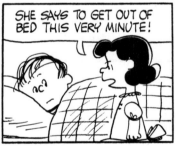

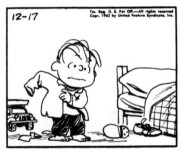

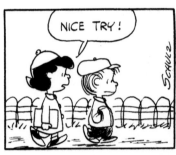

PEANUTS
I'M NOT GOING TO SCHOOL TODAY.. MOM SAID I COULD STAY HOME..
I HAVE A HEADACHE
IF ANY NEW ADVANCEMENTS ARE MADE IN PRIMARY EDUCATION, LET ME KNOW..
HOW POMPOUS CAN YOU GET?
Tm. Reg. U. S. Pat. Off.—All rights reserved
Copr. 1962 by United Feature Syndicate, Inc.
1-7
SCHULZ

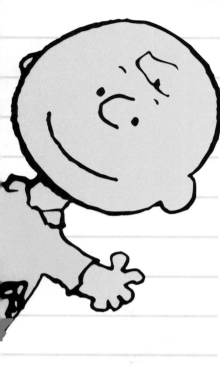

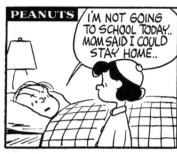

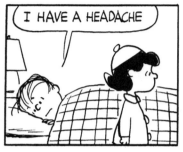

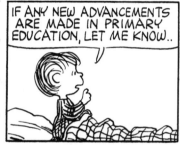

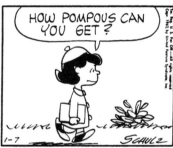

PEANUTS
DID YOU BRING YOUR NOTE?
YOU MEAN MY EXCUSE FOR BEING ABSENT FROM SCHOOL BECAUSE I WAS SICK?
1-8
YES, YOU HAVE TO HAVE ONE.. OTHERWISE THE SCHOOL CAN'T COLLECT ITS STATE-AID MONEY
IS THAT WHAT THE NOTE IS FOR? THAT'S DISILLUSIONING..
Tm. Reg. U. S. Pat. Off.—All rights reserved
Copr. 1963 by United Feature Syndicate, Inc.
I THOUGHT THEY WERE INTERESTED IN WHETHER OR NOT I WAS FEELING BETTER!
SCHULZ

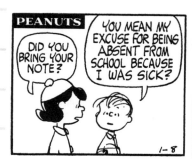

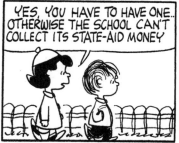

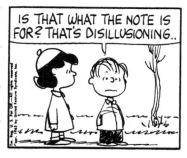

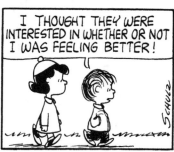

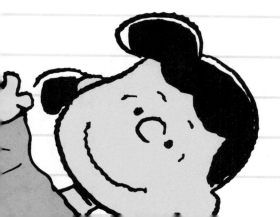

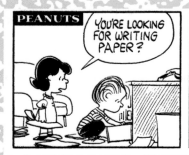

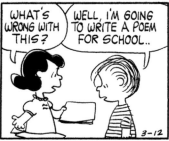

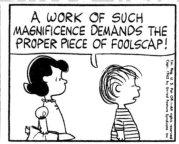

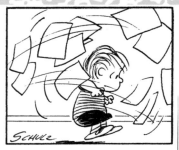

PEANUTS
YOU'RE LOOKING FOR WRITING PAPER?
WHAT'S WRONG WITH THIS?
WELL, I'M GOING TO WRITE A POEM FOR SCHOOL..
3-12
A WORK OF SUCH MAGNIFICENCE DEMANDS THE PROPER PIECE OF FOOLSCAP!
SCHULZ

PEANUTS
Tm. Reg. U.S. Pat. Off.—All rights reserved Copr. 1963 by United Feature Syndicate, Inc.
SCHOOL STARTS MONDAY...
NOT FOR ME!
9-6
WHAT DO YOU MEAN, NOT FOR YOU?
I WENT LAST YEAR!
SCHULZ

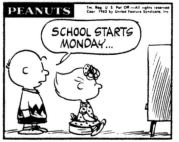

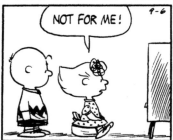

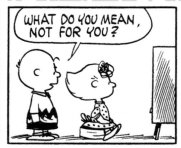

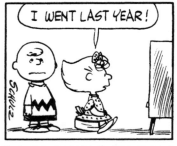

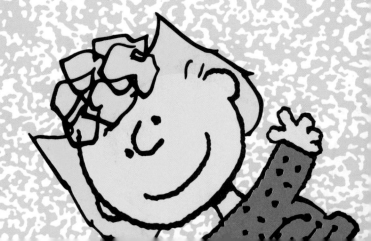

PEANUTS

SO YOU'RE NOT GOING TO SCHOOL MONDAY, HUH, SALLY?

OH, YES, I'M GOING... I CHANGED MY MIND...

9-7

MOM BOUGHT ME A NEW LUNCH BOX..

I FIGURED IF MOM WENT TO ALL THE TROUBLE AND EXPENSE OF GETTING ME A NEW LUNCH BOX, I'D BETTER GO TO SCHOOL...

BUT THAT'S THE ONLY REASON I'M GOING!

PEANUTS

I WOULD LIKE TO SAY I ENJOYED THIS FIRST DAY AT SCHOOL...

I REALIZE THE TEACHERS HAVE PUT IN A LOT OF EFFORT, AND A HOST OF ADMINISTRATORS HAVE WORKED HARD TO DEVELOP OUR CURRENT SCHOLASTIC PROGRAM..

9-9

THE PTA HAS ALSO DONE ITS SHARE AS HAVE THE SCHOOL CUSTODIANS... THEREFORE, I WOULD LIKE VERY MUCH TO SAY I ENJOYED THIS FIRST DAY AT SCHOOL

BUT I DIDN'T!

PEANUTS
STUPID DOG!
9-10
Tm. Reg. U.S. Pat. Off.--All rights reserved
Copr. 1963 by United Feature Syndicate, Inc.
THAT'S HIS, "HA HA..YOU HAVE TO GO TO SCHOOL, AND I DON'T" DANCE!
SCHULZ

PEANUTS
WE'RE SORT OF STUDYING JOURNALISM IN SCHOOL THIS WEEK...
10-16
TODAY OUR TEACHER ASKED US WHAT THE REAL DIFFERENCE IS BETWEEN A MORNING NEWSPAPER AND AN EVENING NEWSPAPER...
I TOLD HER THAT WHEN YOU READ AN EVENING NEWSPAPER, YOU HAVE THE LIGHT ON..
Tm. Reg. U.S. Pat. Off.—All rights reserved
Copr. 1963 by United Feature Syndicate, Inc.
I DIDN'T GET A VERY GOOD GRADE
SCHULZ

PEANUTS
Tm. Reg. U.S. Pat. Off. — All rights reserved
Copr. 1963 by United Feature Syndicate Inc.
I'M WORRIED ABOUT A LITTLE BOY WHO SITS IN FRONT OF ME AT SCHOOL..
12-12
HE CRIES EVERY DAY... THIS AFTERNOON I TRIED TO HELP HIM... I WHACKED HIM ONE ON THE ARM...
YOU WHACKED HIM ONE ON THE ARM?!
I THINK IT HELPED...
THERE'S NOTHING LIKE A LITTLE PHYSICAL PAIN TO TAKE YOUR MIND OFF YOUR EMOTIONAL PROBLEMS..
SCHULZ

PEANUTS
DID THE LITTLE BOY WHO SITS IN FRONT OF YOU AT SCHOOL CRY AGAIN TODAY?
12-13
HE CRIES EVERY DAY! HE HAS ALL THE SIMPLE CHILDHOOD FEARS... FEAR OF BEING LATE FOR SCHOOL, FEAR OF HIS TEACHER, AND FEAR OF THE PRINCIPAL...
FEAR OF NOT KNOWING WHAT ROOM TO GO TO AFTER RECESS, FEAR OF FORGETTING HIS LUNCH, FEAR OF BIGGER KIDS, FEAR OF BEING ASKED TO RECITE...
FEAR OF MISSING THE SCHOOL BUS, FEAR OF NOT KNOWING WHEN TO GET OFF THE SCHOOL BUS, FEAR OF...
SCHULZ
GOOD GRIEF!

PEANUTS

WE HAVE TO WRITE A BOOK REPORT ON "PETER RABBIT" FOR SCHOOL..

I'M GOING TO MAKE A CHARACTER ANALYSIS OF THE FARMER IN THE STORY...YOU KNOW, TRY TO POINT UP HIS BASIC ATTITUDES TOWARD RABBITS, AND SO ON...

I MAY EVEN BRING IN SOME SPECULATIONS ON HIS HOME LIFE WHICH COULD PROVE TO BE QUITE INTERESTING...

ALL IN ALL I HOPE TO UNCOVER SOME NEW TRUTHS ABOUT OUR CULTURE..

I THINK YOU ALREADY HAVE!

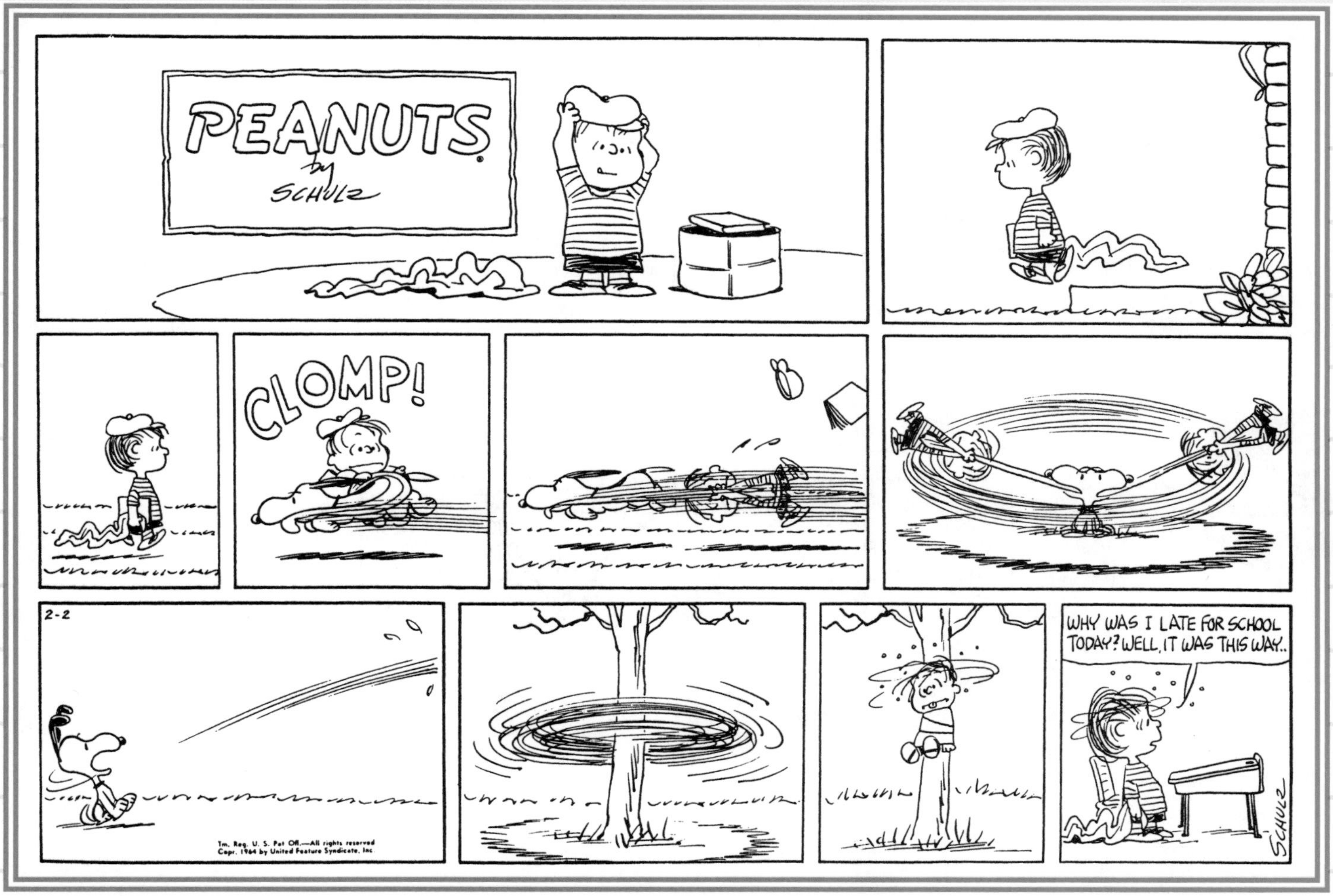
PEANUTS
by
SCHULZ
CLOMP!
2-2
Tm. Reg. U. S. Pat Off.—All rights reserved
Copr. 1964 by United Feature Syndicate, Inc.
WHY WAS I LATE FOR SCHOOL TODAY? WELL, IT WAS THIS WAY..
SCHULZ

PEANUTS
Tm. Reg. U. S. Pat. Off.—All rights reserved
Copr. 1964 by United Feature Syndicate, Inc.
DID YOU HEAR THAT? MY TEACHER SAID, "GOOD MORNING" TO ME!
NOW, I WONDER WHAT SHE MEANT BY THAT? DID SHE REALLY MEAN TO WISH ME "GOOD MORNING"? MAYBE SHE WAS BEING SARCASTIC...
3-23
MAYBE SHE WAS TRYING TO TEACH ME TO BE POLITE... MAYBE SHE THOUGHT SOMEONE FROM THE SCHOOL BOARD WAS LISTENING..
MAYBE WHEN I MEET HER IN THE HALL, IT WOULD BE BEST TO LOOK THE OTHER WAY..
SCHULZ

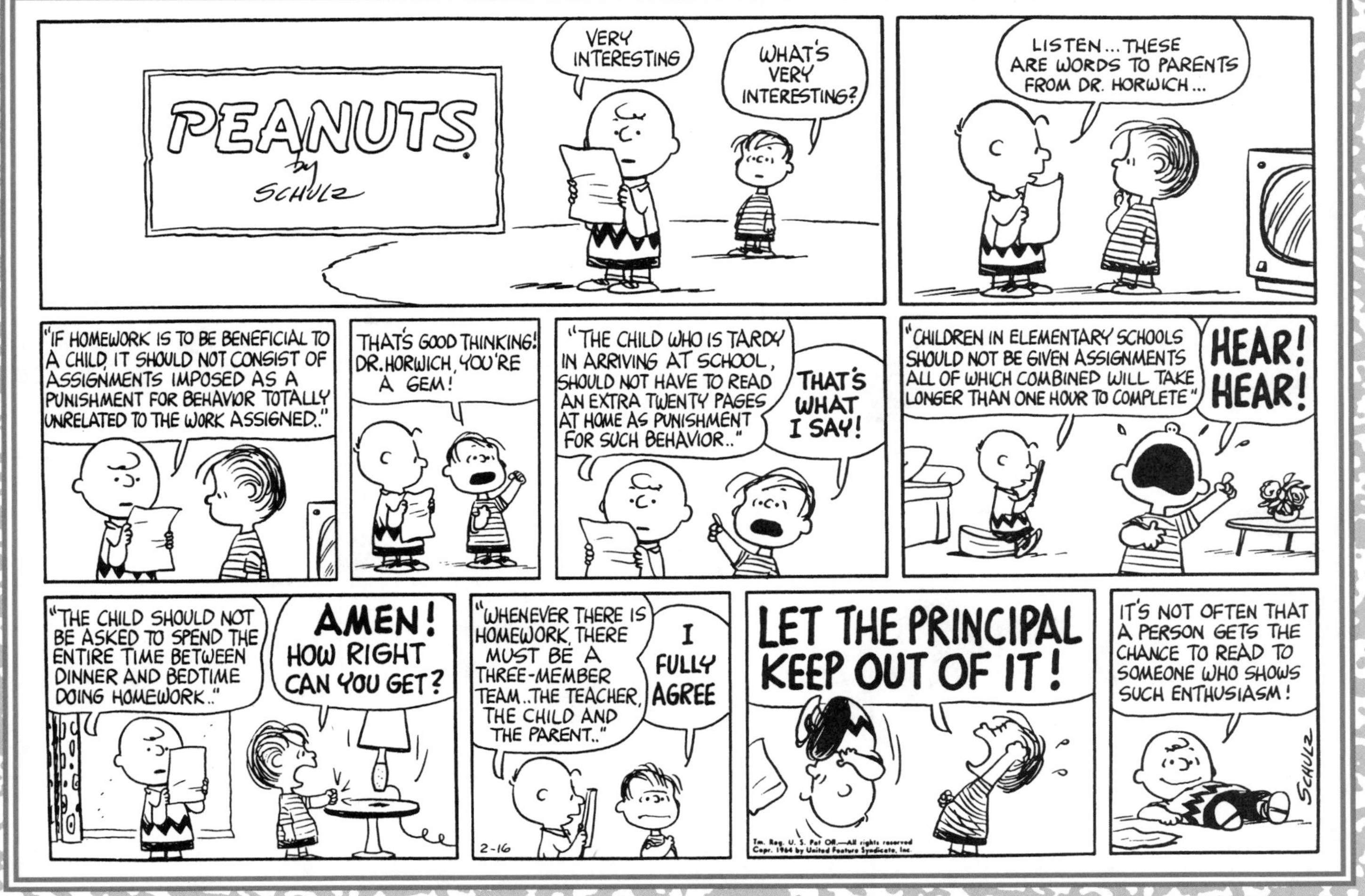
PEANUTS
by SCHULZ
VERY INTERESTING
WHAT'S VERY INTERESTING?
LISTEN... THESE ARE WORDS TO PARENTS FROM DR. HORWICH...
"IF HOMEWORK IS TO BE BENEFICIAL TO A CHILD, IT SHOULD NOT CONSIST OF ASSIGNMENTS IMPOSED AS A PUNISHMENT FOR BEHAVIOR TOTALLY UNRELATED TO THE WORK ASSIGNED.."
THAT'S GOOD THINKING! DR. HORWICH, YOU'RE A GEM!
"THE CHILD WHO IS TARDY IN ARRIVING AT SCHOOL, SHOULD NOT HAVE TO READ AN EXTRA TWENTY PAGES AT HOME AS PUNISHMENT FOR SUCH BEHAVIOR.."
THAT'S WHAT I SAY!
"CHILDREN IN ELEMENTARY SCHOOLS SHOULD NOT BE GIVEN ASSIGNMENTS ALL OF WHICH COMBINED WILL TAKE LONGER THAN ONE HOUR TO COMPLETE"
HEAR! HEAR!
"THE CHILD SHOULD NOT BE ASKED TO SPEND THE ENTIRE TIME BETWEEN DINNER AND BEDTIME DOING HOMEWORK.."
AMEN! HOW RIGHT CAN YOU GET?
"WHENEVER THERE IS HOMEWORK, THERE MUST BE A THREE-MEMBER TEAM..THE TEACHER, THE CHILD AND THE PARENT.."
I FULLY AGREE
2-16
LET THE PRINCIPAL KEEP OUT OF IT!
Tm. Reg. U. S. Pat. Off.—All rights reserved Copr. 1964 by United Feature Syndicate, Inc.
IT'S NOT OFTEN THAT A PERSON GETS THE CHANCE TO READ TO SOMEONE WHO SHOWS SUCH ENTHUSIASM!
SCHULZ

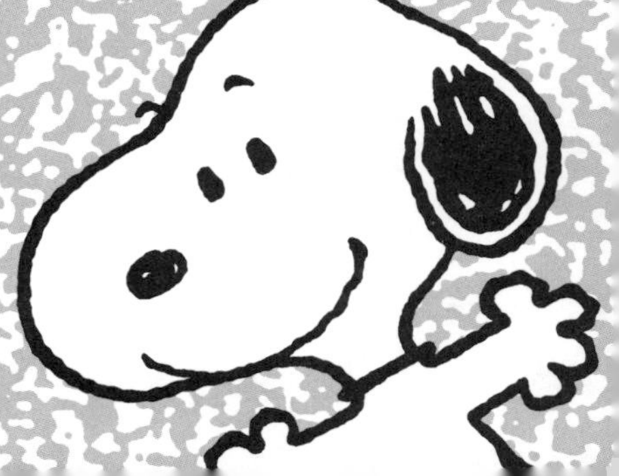

PEANUTS I DIDN'T FEEL VERY WELL WHEN I GOT UP THIS MORNING..

MY MOTHER ALMOST KEPT ME HOME FROM SCHOOL..

FINALLY, SHE DECIDED I'D BETTER GO..

YOU LOOKED LIKE YOU WERE FEELING BETTER, HUH?

4-3

NO, SHE HAD MY LUNCH ALL MADE!

PEANUTS I'M GOING TO BE **WHAT**?

YOU'RE GOING TO BE MY SCIENCE PROJECT!

4-14

I'M GOING TO ENTER YOU IN OUR SCHOOL SCIENCE FAIR..

I'M GOING TO MAKE A SERIES OF TESTS WITH YOU AND THAT STUPID BLANKET TO SEE WHY IT BRINGS YOU SECURITY..

SUDDENLY I FEEL VERY **INSECURE**!

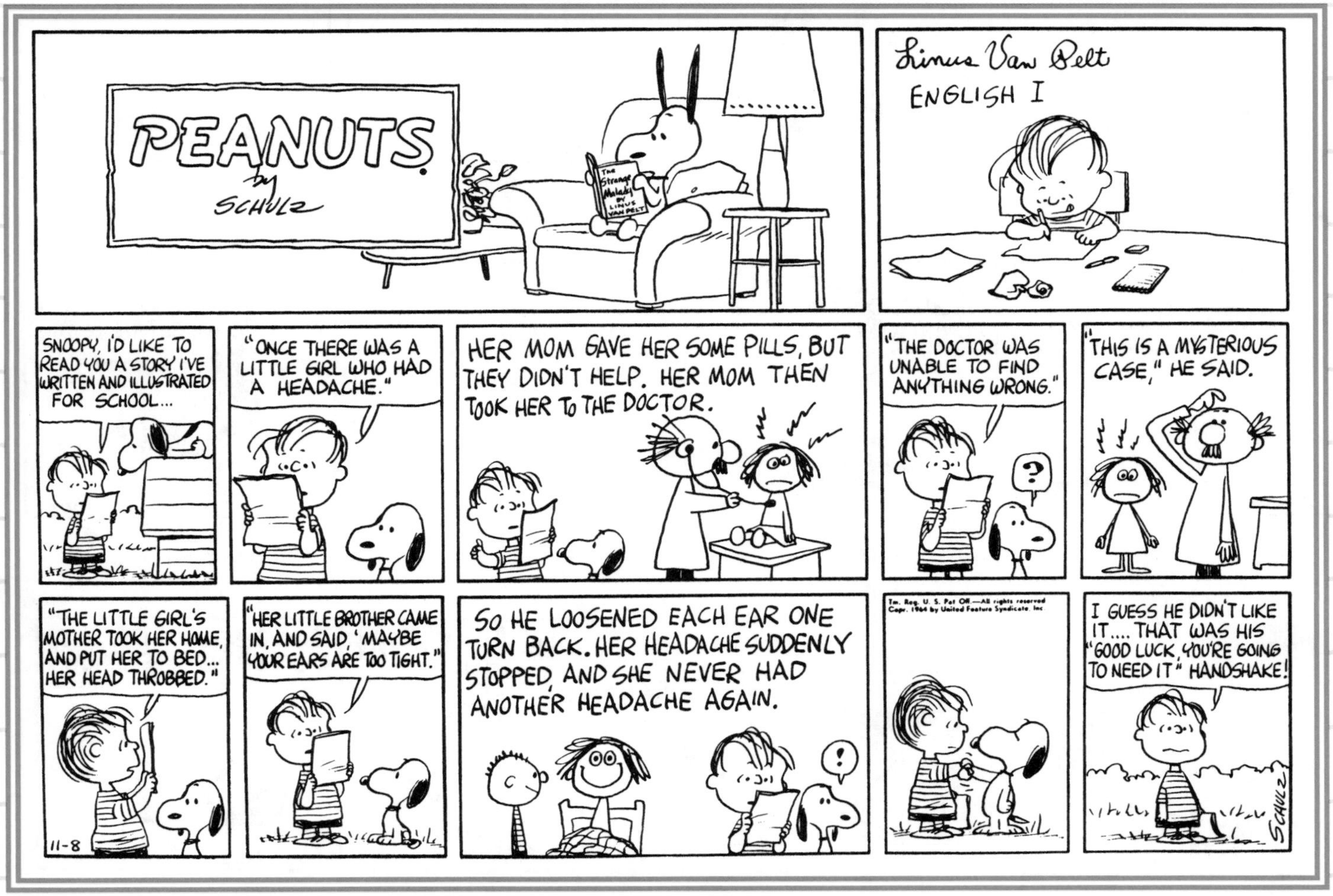
PEANUTS
by SCHULZ
The Strange Malady BY LINUS VAN PELT
Linus Van Pelt
ENGLISH I
SNOOPY, I'D LIKE TO READ YOU A STORY I'VE WRITTEN AND ILLUSTRATED FOR SCHOOL...
"ONCE THERE WAS A LITTLE GIRL WHO HAD A HEADACHE."
HER MOM GAVE HER SOME PILLS, BUT THEY DIDN'T HELP. HER MOM THEN TOOK HER TO THE DOCTOR.
"THE DOCTOR WAS UNABLE TO FIND ANYTHING WRONG."
?
"THIS IS A MYSTERIOUS CASE," HE SAID.
"THE LITTLE GIRL'S MOTHER TOOK HER HOME, AND PUT HER TO BED... HER HEAD THROBBED."
11-8
"HER LITTLE BROTHER CAME IN, AND SAID, 'MAYBE YOUR EARS ARE TOO TIGHT.'"
SO HE LOOSENED EACH EAR ONE TURN BACK. HER HEADACHE SUDDENLY STOPPED, AND SHE NEVER HAD ANOTHER HEADACHE AGAIN.
!
Tm. Reg. U. S. Pat Off.—All rights reserved
Copr. 1964 by United Feature Syndicate, Inc
I GUESS HE DIDN'T LIKE IT.... THAT WAS HIS "GOOD LUCK, YOU'RE GOING TO NEED IT" HANDSHAKE!
SCHULZ

PEANUTS

DON'T TELL ME THAT'S YOUR LUNCH?!

SOME OF IT...

WHAT ELSE DO YOU HAVE IN THERE?

MY SKATE BOARD!

3-30

PEANUTS

MY ESSAY? YES, MA'AM... I HAVE IT RIGHT HERE..

BUT I COULDN'T WRITE A THOUSAND WORDS.... I ONLY WROTE EIGHT..

DETAIL? WELL, YES, I SUPPOSE I COULD HAVE GONE INTO MORE DETAIL...

BUT WITH THE KIND OF SUMMERS I HAVE, IT'S BEST TO TRY TO FORGET THE DETAILS

9-16

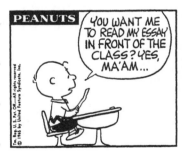

PEANUTS

YOU WANT ME TO READ MY ESSAY IN FRONT OF THE CLASS? YES, MA'AM...

"WHAT I DID THIS SUMMER... I WENT TO CAMP, AND I PLAYED BALL.........THE END"

HA HA HA HA HA HA HA HA

I LOVE SCHOOL...IT'S SUCH A SATISFYING EXPERIENCE!

9-17

SCHULZ

48

PEANUTS
Tm. Reg. U.S. Pat. Off.—All rights reserved ©1966 by United Feature Syndicate, Inc.
WE LEARNED IN SCHOOL TODAY THAT THERE ARE SIXTEEN OZZES IN A LIB..
WE'VE BEEN STUDYING PINTS AND QUARTS, AND FEET AND INCHES AND OZZES AND LIBS...
3-10
I GET KIND OF CONFUSED ON QUARTS AND FEET, BUT I'M GOOD ON OZZES AND LIBS..
DID YOU KNOW THERE ARE SIXTEEN OZZES IN A LIB?
I NEVER KNOW HOW TO ANSWER A QUESTION LIKE THAT..
SCHULZ

PEANUTS
Tm. Reg. U.S. Pat. Off.—All rights reserved ©1966 by United Feature Syndicate, Inc.
WHAT'S THIS? THAT LITTLE RED-HAIRED GIRL DROPPED HER PENCIL...
GEE... IT'S GOT TEETH MARKS ALL OVER IT...
SHE NIBBLES ON HER PENCIL...
SHE'S HUMAN!
SCHULZ
3-25

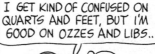

PEANUTS
WE HAD A GOOD TIME AT SCHOOL TODAY..
Tm. Reg. U.S. Pat. Off.—All rights reserved ©1966 by United Feature Syndicate, Inc.
OUR TEACHER TOOK US ON A FIELD TRIP...WE WENT OUT, AND WE SAW THIS GREAT BIG FIELD
4-28
IT WAS A REAL FIELD, AND WE SAW IT! WE STOOD RIGHT THERE, AND WE SAW THAT FIELD!
DO YOU THINK YOU'LL BE GOING ON ANY MORE FIELD TRIPS?
I DOUBT IT..WHEN YOU'VE SEEN ONE FIELD, YOU'VE SEEN THEM ALL
SCHULZ

PEANUTS
IS YOUR MOM PUTTING NOTES IN YOUR LUNCH AGAIN?
YES, THIS IS THE FIRST ONE THIS YEAR
"DEAR SON, I WILL BE AWAY WHEN YOU GET HOME FROM SCHOOL TODAY.. I HAVE BEEN INVITED TO A BRIDGE PARTY... I WILL LEAVE A SANDWICH AND SOME MILK IN THE REFRIGERATOR..."
"STUDY HARD TODAY..MAKE US PROUD OF YOU..THE FUTURE IS IN THE HANDS OF YOUR GENERATION..I SUPPOSE IN MANY WAYS OUR GENERATION HAS FAILED YOURS, BUT WE DID TRY... PLEASE JUDGE US WITH MERCY.."
9-13
MOM GETS CARRIED AWAY!
Tm. Reg. U.S. Pat. Off.—All rights reserved ©1966 by United Feature Syndicate, Inc
SCHULZ

PEANUTS
Tm. Reg. U.S. Pat. Off.—All rights reserved ©1966 by United Feature Syndicate, Inc
I FEEL KIND OF DIZZY...
9-14
MAYBE YOU SHOULDN'T GO TO SCHOOL...MAYBE YOU SHOULD STAY HOME
I CAN'T
HOW CAN MISSING ONE DAY HURT YOU?
I MIGHT NOT GET TO GO TO THE COLLEGE OF MY CHOICE!
SCHULZ

PEANUTS
I DON'T SEE HOW YOU REMEMBER YOUR LOCKER COMBINATION, CHARLIE BROWN
IT'S EASY...3-24-7....SEE?
BUT HOW IN THE WORLD DO YOU REMEMBER IT?
BABE RUTH WAS NUMBER 3, WILLIE MAYS IS NUMBER 24 AND MICKEY MANTLE IS NUMBER 7!
SCHULZ
10-11

PEANUTS
MOM PUT A NOTE IN MY LUNCH TODAY..
"DEAR SON, I HOPE YOU ENJOY THE LUNCH I MADE FOR YOU TODAY.. STUDY HARD...IT IS IMPORTANT TO BE A GOOD STUDENT..."
12-7
"HOWEVER, DO NOT NEGLECT YOUR PEER-GROUP RATING"
WHEN SHE WAS YOUNG, MOM NEVER FELT SHE HAD A VERY GOOD PEER-GROUP RATING...
SCHULZ

PEANUTS
I ALMOST GOT AN "A" ON MY SPELLING TEST
3/31
THE ONLY WORD I MISSED WAS "CUCUMBER"
DON'T WORRY ABOUT IT..
Tm. Reg. U.S. Pat. Off.—All rights reserved
© 1967 by United Feature Syndicate, Inc.
THE WAY I SEE IT, A WORD LIKE "CUCUMBER" **DESERVES** TO BE MISSPELLED!
SCHULZ

PEANUTS
SCHOOL STARTS AGAIN IN NINE DAYS...
AAUGHHH!!!
RIP!
8-26
good grief!
Tm. Reg. U.S. Pat. Off.—All rights reserved
© 1967 by United Feature Syndicate, Inc.
SCHULZ
THAT'S THE ONLY NEWS WHICH COULD CAUSE ME TO REND MY GARMENT!

PEANUTS
I'M IN NO SHAPE FOR THE FIRST DAY OF SCHOOL...
9-5
I CAN'T LIVE WITHOUT THAT BLANKET...I HAVEN'T SLEPT IN A WEEK... BESIDES, HOW CAN I GO TO SCHOOL WHEN I...
KLUNK!
Tm. Reg. U. S. Pat. Off.—All rights reserved © 1967 by United Feature Syndicate, Inc.
..KEEP PASSING OUT ?
SCHULZ

PEANUTS
WHY WAS I LATE FOR SCHOOL, MA'AM ?
Tm. Reg. U. S. Pat. Off.—All rights reserved ©1967 by United Feature Syndicate, Inc.
9-6
WELL, IT WAS ON ACCOUNT OF A BLANKET WHICH I DON'T HAVE, AND I PASSED OUT FOUR TIMES ON THE WAY TO SCHOOL, AND THAT SORT OF HELD ME UP AND....
NO, MA'AM, I'M NOT EXACTLY SICK, BUT GRAMMA GAVE UP SMOKING, AND I LACK SECURITY, AND.... YES, MA'AM?
YOU DON'T UNDERSTAND ? NO, I DON'T SUPPOSE YOU DO...
SIGH
SCHULZ

PEANUTS
WE'RE HAVING A TEST TODAY ON CHAPTER FOUR..
CHAPTER **FOUR**?! GOOD GRIEF, I STUDIED CHAPTER TWO!
I'M DOOMED...
© 1968 by United Feature Syndicate, Inc.
Tm. Reg. U. S. Pat. Off.—All rights reserved
1/23
STUDYING THE WRONG CHAPTER IS LIKE CUTTING YOUR FINGERNAILS TOO SHORT!
SCHULZ

PEANUTS
Tm. Reg. U. S. Pat. Off.—All rights reserved
© 1968 by United Feature Syndicate, Inc.
I WOULD HAVE MADE A GOOD SCHOOL PRINCIPAL!
1-30
SCHULZ

PEANUTS
MOM PUT A NOTE IN MY LUNCH AGAIN, I SEE...
"DEAR SON, I HOPE YOU WILL STUDY HARD IN SUMMER SCHOOL.. DO NOT LOOK UPON IT AS A PUNISHMENT, BUT RATHER AS A PRIVILEGE..."
"WE ARE VERY PROUD OF YOU, AND WANT YOU TO HAVE A GOOD EDUCATION"
Tm. Reg. U.S. Pat. Off.—All rights reserved © 1968 by United Feature Syndicate, Inc.
"THIS NOTE WILL SELF-DESTRUCT IN FIVE SECONDS!"
POOF!
SCHULZ

PEANUTS
Tm. Reg. U.S. Pat. Off.—All rights reserved © 1968 by United Feature Syndicate, Inc.
MISS OTHMAR?
WOULD YOU PLEASE REPEAT OUR HOMEWORK ASSIGNMENT?
9-4
"WRITE A TWO-PAGE THEME ON WHAT WE DID THIS SUMMER"
HOW DO YOU TEACHERS KEEP COMING UP WITH THESE GREAT NEW IDEAS?
SCHULZ

PEANUTS
YOU LOOK WORRIED...
I AM WORRIED! WE'RE HAVING A TEST IN SCHOOL TOMORROW, AND THERE'S NO WAY I CAN PASS IT... ABSOLUTELY NO WAY!
9-30
HAVE YOU TRIED STUDYING?
Tm. Reg. U.S. Pat. Off.—All rights reserved © 1968 by United Feature Syndicate, Inc.
WE'RE HAVING A TEST IN SCHOOL TOMORROW, AND THERE'S NO WAY I CAN PASS IT... ABSOLUTELY NO WAY!
SCHULZ

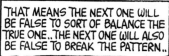

PEANUTS
LET'S SEE NOW... IN A TRUE OR FALSE TEST, THE FIRST QUESTION IS ALMOST ALWAYS 'TRUE'...
10-3
THAT MEANS THE NEXT ONE WILL BE FALSE TO SORT OF BALANCE THE TRUE ONE.. THE NEXT ONE WILL ALSO BE FALSE TO BREAK THE PATTERN..
THEN ANOTHER TRUE AND THEN TWO MORE FALSE ONES AND THEN THREE TRUES IN A ROW... THEY ALWAYS HAVE THREE TRUES IN A ROW SOME PLACE... THEN ANOTHER FALSE AND ANOTHER TRUE...
Tm. Reg. U. S. Pat. Off.—All rights reserved © 1968 by United Feature Syndicate, Inc.
IF YOU'RE SMART, YOU CAN PASS A TRUE OR FALSE TEST WITHOUT BEING SMART!
SCHULZ

PEANUTS
Tm. Reg. U. S. Pat. Off.—All rights reserved © 1968 by United Feature Syndicate, Inc.
10-21
I WONDER IF HE'S AUDITING THIS COURSE, OR TAKING IT FOR CREDIT...
SCHULZ

PEANUTS
I COULD HAVE GONE TO SCHOOL, AND BECOME EDUCATED..
10-26
I COULD HAVE STUDIED THE "ODYSSEY" AND "LORD JIM" AND "BLEAK HOUSE"
Tm. Reg. U.S. Pat. Off.—All rights reserved © 1968 by United Feature Syndicate, Inc.
BUT JUST BECAUSE I'M A DOG THEY SAY I CAN'T GO TO THEIR STUPID SCHOOL
I WOULD HAVE BEEN GREAT AT THE SENIOR PROM!
SCHULZ

PEANUTS
NUMBERS ARE BEAUTIFUL..
12-4
I LIKE TWOS THE BEST...THEY'RE SORT OF GENTLE..THREES AND FIVES ARE MEAN, BUT A FOUR IS ALWAYS PLEASANT..I LIKE SEVENS AND EIGHTS, TOO, BUT NINES ALWAYS SCARE ME...TENS ARE GREAT...
HAVE YOU DONE THOSE DIVISION PROBLEMS FOR TOMORROW?
NOTHING SPOILS NUMBERS FASTER THAN A LOT OF ARITHMETIC!
Tm. Reg. U. S. Pat. Off.—All rights reserved
© 1968 by United Feature Syndicate, Inc.
SCHULZ

PEANUTS
Tm. Reg. U. S. Pat. Off.—All rights reserved © 1969 by United Feature Syndicate, Inc.
2-13
YES, MA'AM... THANK YOU...I'LL BE VERY HAPPY TO DO IT...
EACH DAY OUR TEACHER SELECTS ONE BOY IN OUR CLASS TO GO OUTSIDE AND POUND ALL THE ERASERS.. IT'S CONSIDERED A GREAT HONOR TO BE CHOSEN FOR THIS TASK...
POUND POUND GASP POUND GASP POUND POUND GASP
I COULD DIE FROM ALL THIS HONOR!
SCHULZ

PEANUTS
Tm. Reg. U. S. Pat. Off.—All rights reserved © 1969 by United Feature Syndicate, Inc.
I WONDER IF MISS OTHMAR WILL ASK YOU TO POUND ERASERS AGAIN TODAY...
I DON'T THINK YOU SHOULD BE INHALING ALL THAT CHALK DUST, CHARLIE BROWN..
WHAT DO YOU THINK?
2-19
SCHULZ

PEANUTS
I'M GOING OVER TO THE PENCIL SHARPENER..THIS LEAD BROKE...
ACTUALLY, IT ISN'T LEAD AT ALL.. IT'S A COMBINATION OF BAVARIAN CLAY AND MADAGASCAR GRAPHITE
4-21
Tm. Reg. U. S. Pat. Off.—All rights reserved
© 1969 by United Feature Syndicate, Inc.
YOU'RE THE ONLY PERSON I KNOW WHO CAN TAKE THE JOY OUT OF SHARPENING A PENCIL!
SCHULZ

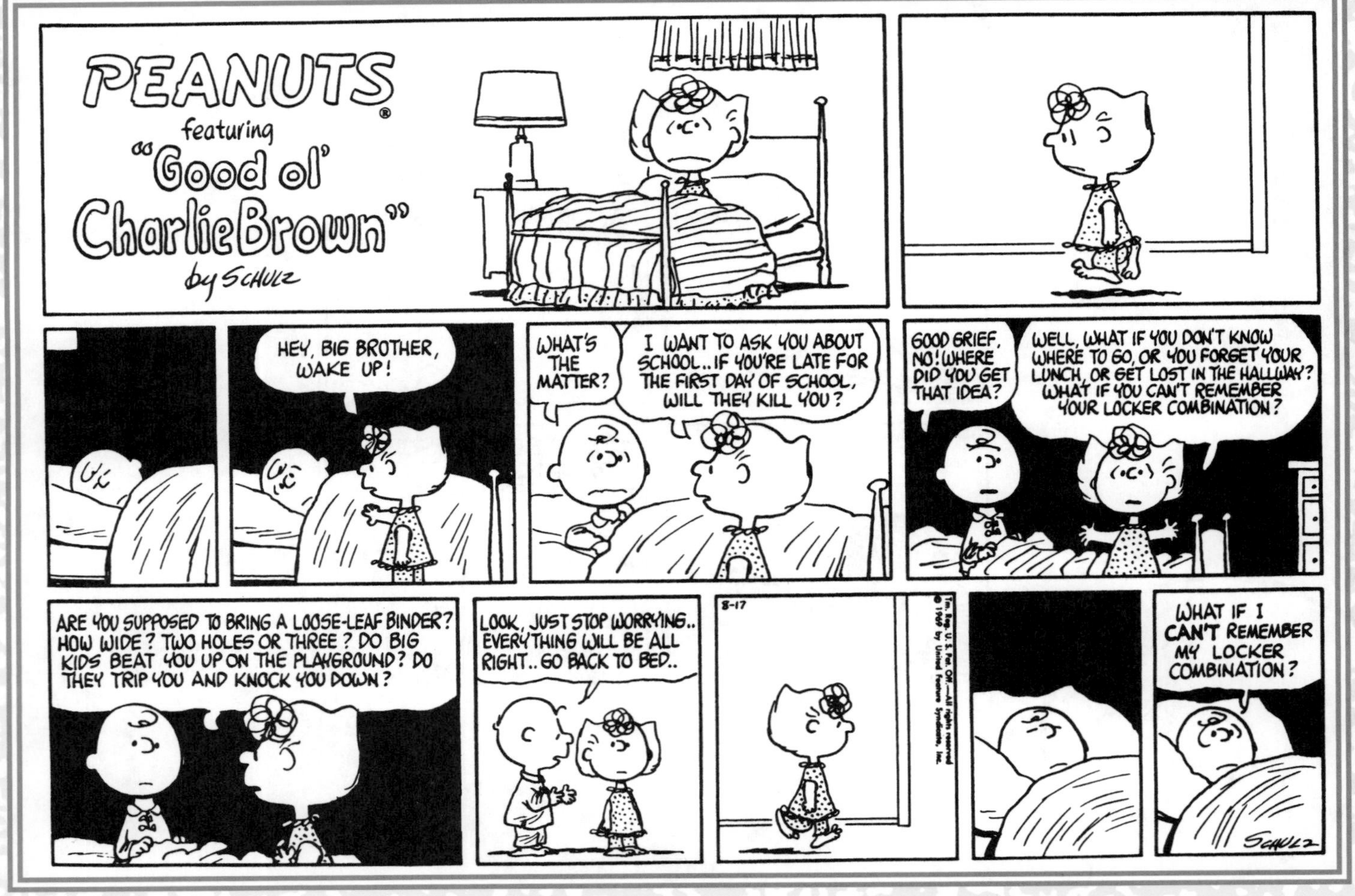
PEANUTS®
featuring "Good ol' CharlieBrown"
by SCHULZ
HEY, BIG BROTHER, WAKE UP!
WHAT'S THE MATTER?
I WANT TO ASK YOU ABOUT SCHOOL.. IF YOU'RE LATE FOR THE FIRST DAY OF SCHOOL, WILL THEY KILL YOU?
GOOD GRIEF, NO! WHERE DID YOU GET THAT IDEA?
WELL, WHAT IF YOU DON'T KNOW WHERE TO GO, OR YOU FORGET YOUR LUNCH, OR GET LOST IN THE HALLWAY? WHAT IF YOU CAN'T REMEMBER YOUR LOCKER COMBINATION?
ARE YOU SUPPOSED TO BRING A LOOSE-LEAF BINDER? HOW WIDE? TWO HOLES OR THREE? DO BIG KIDS BEAT YOU UP ON THE PLAYGROUND? DO THEY TRIP YOU AND KNOCK YOU DOWN?
LOOK, JUST STOP WORRYING.. EVERYTHING WILL BE ALL RIGHT.. GO BACK TO BED..
8-17
Tm. Reg. U.S. Pat. Off.—All rights reserved © 1969 by United Feature Syndicate, Inc.
WHAT IF I CAN'T REMEMBER MY LOCKER COMBINATION?
SCHULZ

PEANUTS
THIS IS IT
IT'S THE FIRST DAY OF SCHOOL!!
9-2
PUT ON THE BOILED EGGS! SHINE YOUR SHOES! MAKE YOUR LUNCH! CONJUGATE YOUR VERBS!
Tm. Reg. U. S. Pat. Off.—All rights reserved © 1969 by United Feature Syndicate, Inc.
"CONJUGATE YOUR VERBS"?
SCHULZ

PEANUTS
BOY, DID YOU EVER GOOF ME UP!
YOU HAD ME TAKE MY LUNCH TO SCHOOL IN A LUNCH BOX... DO YOU KNOW WHAT HAPPENED?
9-3
Tm. Reg. U.S. Pat. Off.—All rights reserved © 1969 by United Feature Syndicate, Inc.
ALL THE OTHER KIDS WERE BROWN-BAGGING IT!! I FELT LIKE A FOOL!
YOU GAVE ME BAD ADVICE, BIG BROTHER!
I CAN'T STAND ALL THIS RESPONSIBILITY..
SCHULZ

PEANUTS
YES, MA'AM? MY NAME?
9-4
MY NAME IS SALLY BROWN, AND I HATE SCHOOL!
Tm. Reg. U.S. Pat. Off.—All rights reserved © 1969 by United Feature Syndicate, Inc.
PLEASE, DON'T CRY...
SCHULZ

PEANUTS
Tm. Reg. U.S. Pat. Off.—All rights reserved © 1969 by United Feature Syndicate, Inc.
I HATE SCHOOL!
IT'S DRIVING ME CRAZY!!!
AS SOON AS I LEARN ONE THING, THEY GO ON TO SOMETHING ELSE!
10-1
I FINALLY LEARNED WHERE I'M SUPPOSED TO EAT LUNCH, AND NOW THEY EXPECT ME TO KNOW WHERE MY DESK IS!
SCHULZ

PEANUTS
Tm. Reg. U.S. Pat. Off.—All rights reserved © 1969 by United Feature Syndicate, Inc.
DRAW A FARM? YOU WANT US TO DRAW A FARM?
I CAN'T DRAW A FARM.. I'VE NEVER EVEN **SEEN** A FARM! BESIDES, COWS' LEGS ARE IMPOSSIBLE TO DRAW...
I DEFY ANYONE IN THIS CLASS TO DRAW A GOOD COW LEG!
10-2
I'M THE ONLY PERSON I KNOW WHO'S FAILING FIRST-GRADE ART..
PRINCIPAL'S OFFICE
SCHULZ

PEANUTS
Tm. Reg. U.S. Pat. Off.—All rights reserved © 1969 by United Feature Syndicate, Inc.
I LEARNED SOMETHING IN SCHOOL TODAY
I SIGNED UP FOR FOLK GUITAR, COMPUTER PROGRAMMING, STAINED GLASS ART, SHOEMAKING AND A NATURAL FOODS WORKSHOP..
11-10
I GOT SPELLING, HISTORY, ARITHMETIC AND TWO STUDY PERIODS
SO WHAT DID YOU LEARN?
I LEARNED THAT WHAT YOU SIGN UP FOR AND WHAT YOU GET ARE TWO DIFFERENT THINGS
SCHULZ

PEANUTS
Tm. Reg. U.S. Pat. Off.—All rights reserved © 1969 by United Feature Syndicate, Inc.
MISS SWANSON, I DON'T UNDERSTAND THE FOURTH PROBLEM
12-8
OF COURSE, I DON'T REALLY UNDERSTAND THE OTHER THREE PROBLEMS, EITHER...
ACTUALLY, I DON'T UNDERSTAND MATH AT ALL
LET'S FACE IT... I DON'T EVEN UNDERSTAND SCHOOL!
SCHULZ

PEANUTS

NOW, THAT'S WHAT I CALL A BOOK REPORT..

THIS TIME I REALLY OUTDID MYSELF

I'VE GOT THE AUTHOR'S NAME, A BRIEF DESCRIPTION OF THE PLOT AND EVERYTHING...

I EVEN READ THE BOOK!

PEANUTS

SCHOOL STARTS NEXT WEEK

WHERE AM I GOING TO GET THREE DOLLARS FOR ANOTHER DESK?

YOU DON'T HAVE TO BUY YOUR OWN DESK! WHERE'D YOU GET THAT IDEA?

REALLY?

JUST WAIT 'TIL I CATCH THE KID WHO SOLD ME THAT ONE LAST YEAR!

PEANUTS

WHY DO I HAVE TO GO TO SCHOOL AND LEARN THE NAMES OF ALL THOSE RIVERS?

I'VE NEVER EVEN **SEEN** A RIVER! THEY COULD AT LEAST TAKE ME TO **SEE** A RIVER!

YOU HAVE A GOOD POINT THERE..

AND MOUNTAINS! I'VE NEVER SEEN A MOUNTAIN! OR A KING! OR EVEN A CAPITAL CITY!

AND WE'RE SUPPOSED TO KNOW ALL THOSE BORDERS! I'VE NEVER **SEEN** A BORDER!

THIS MAY TAKE MORE THAN ONE FIELD TRIP TO THE ZOO..

66

PEANUTS
SCHOOL!
TODAY'S THE FIRST DAY OF SCHOOL! MEMORIZE THOSE CONJUNCTIONS! NAME THOSE RIVERS!
Tm. Reg. U. S. Pat. Off.—All rights reserved © 1970 by United Feature Syndicate, Inc.
DON'T FORGET YOUR LOCKER COMBINATION!! WHAT'S THE CAPITAL OF VENEZUELA?!
9-8
I THINK THE SUMMERS ARE GETTING SHORTER..
SCHULZ

PEANUTS
WELL, HOW WAS YOUR FIRST DAY OF SCHOOL?
I KNEW YOU'D ASK ME THAT!
EVERYONE ALWAYS ASKS HOW THE FIRST DAY OF SCHOOL WAS! WHO CARES?
9-9
IT'S THE LAST DAY OF SCHOOL THAT COUNTS! IT'S THAT FINAL REPORT! IT'S THAT OL' DIPLOMA!
IT'S THAT OL' GRADE! IT'S THAT OL' SHEEPSKIN! IT'S..
SIGH

PEANUTS
English Theme
"If I Had a Pony"
If I had a pony, I'd saddle up and ride so far from this school it would make your head swim.
Tm. Reg. U. S. Pat. Off.—All rights reserved © 1970 by United Feature Syndicate, Inc
9-29
THAT'S A GOOD WAY TO GET A "D-MINUS"!
SCHULZ

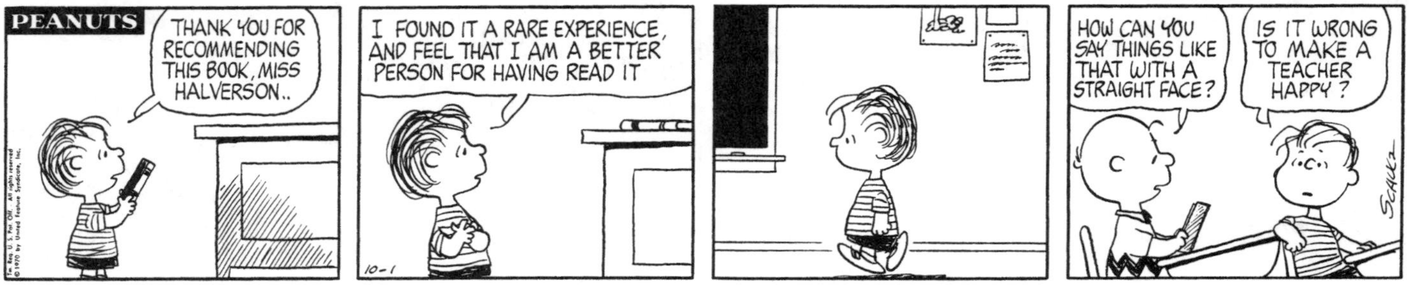
PEANUTS
THANK YOU FOR RECOMMENDING THIS BOOK, MISS HALVERSON..
I FOUND IT A RARE EXPERIENCE, AND FEEL THAT I AM A BETTER PERSON FOR HAVING READ IT
10-1
HOW CAN YOU SAY THINGS LIKE THAT WITH A STRAIGHT FACE?
IS IT WRONG TO MAKE A TEACHER HAPPY?
SCHULZ

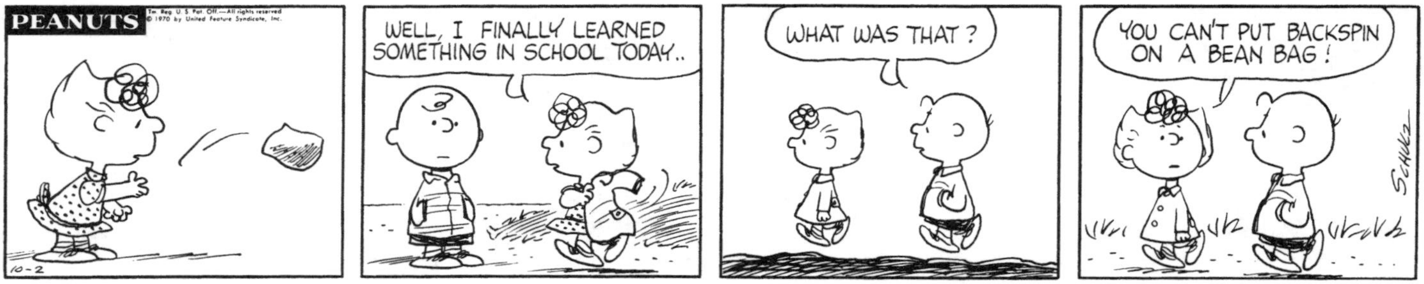
PEANUTS
Tm. Reg. U.S. Pat. Off.—All rights reserved © 1970 by United Feature Syndicate, Inc.
10-2
WELL, I FINALLY LEARNED SOMETHING IN SCHOOL TODAY..
WHAT WAS THAT?
YOU CAN'T PUT BACKSPIN ON A BEAN BAG!
SCHULZ

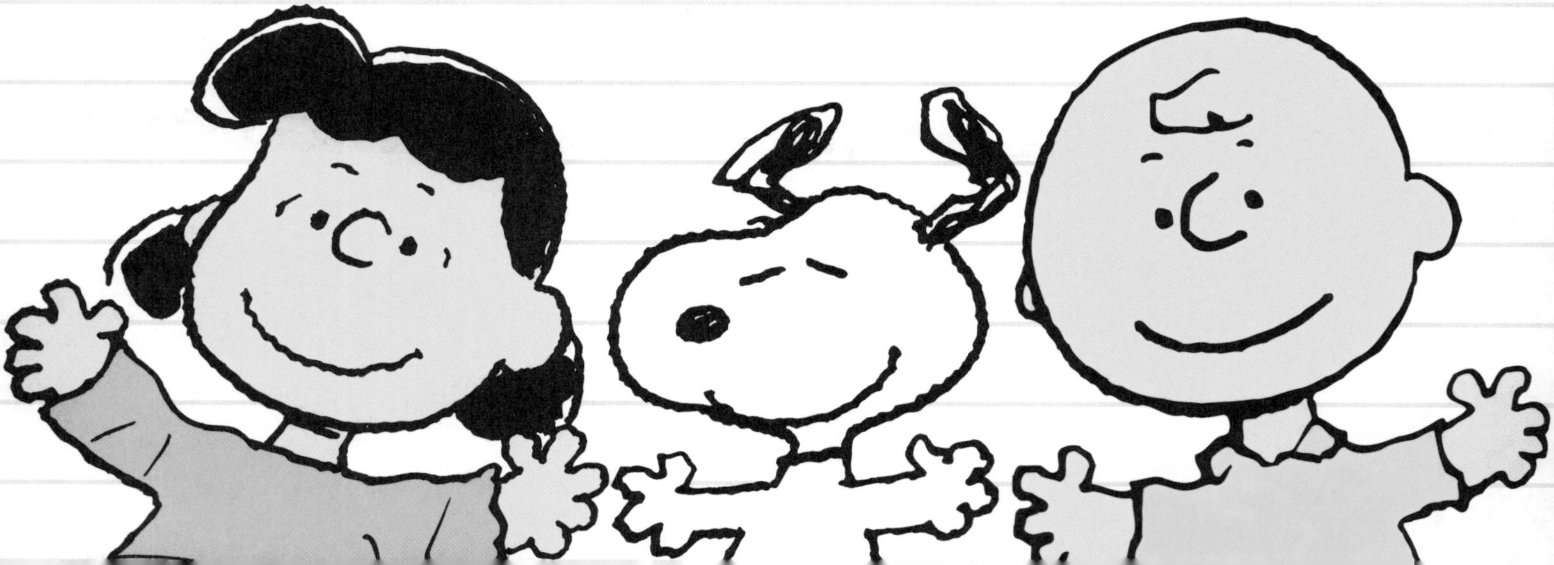

PEANUTS
I'LL NEVER GET THIS SECOND PROBLEM
JUST PUT DOWN "ELEVEN," FRANKLIN, AND DON'T WORRY ABOUT IT... THAT'S WHAT I DID..
2-8
Tm. Reg. U. S. Pat. Off.—All rights reserved © 1971 by United Feature Syndicate, Inc.
"X" IS ALMOST ALWAYS ELEVEN, AND "Y" IS ALMOST ALWAYS NINE...
ONE THING I'VE LEARNED ABOUT ALGEBRA..DON'T TAKE IT TOO SERIOUSLY...
SCHULZ

PEANUTS
A SCIENCE PROJECT?
Tm. Reg. U. S. Pat. Off.—All rights reserved © 1971 by United Feature Syndicate, Inc.
OH, GOOD GRIEF! I HATE SCIENCE PROJECTS...I CAN NEVER THINK OF ANYTHING DIFFERENT...
I'M GOING TO DO MINE ON THE VARIOUS KINDS OF METALS IN THE EARTH AND HOW EACH HAS AFFECTED THE PROGRESS OF MANKIND...
2-9
SCHULZ
MAYBE I'LL DO ONE ON STOMACH ACHES

PEANUTS
PROBLEM, CHUCK..
Tm. Reg. U.S. Pat. Off.—All rights reserved © 1971 by United Feature Syndicate, Inc.
THEY WANT ANOTHER ONE OF THOSE SCIENCE PROJECT THINGS AT SCHOOL...GOT ANY IDEAS? NO, DON'T TELL ME..I HAVE TO WORK THIS OUT MYSELF...
2-10
A SCIENCE PROJECT IS ONLY GOOD IF YOU DO IT COMPLETELY BY YOURSELF..THANKS ANYWAY, CHUCK
SIGH
SCHULZ

PEANUTS
MY SCIENCE PROJECT? YES, MA'AM..I HAVE IT READY TO SHOW TO THE CLASS..
2-11
AT FIRST I HAD A LITTLE TROUBLE TRYING TO DECIDE WHAT TO DO, BUT HERE IT IS......
TOAST!!
science PRoject
Tm. Reg. U.S. Pat. Off.—All rights reserved © 1971 by United Feature Syndicate, Inc.
SCHULZ

PEANUTS
Tm. Reg. U.S. Pat. Off.—All rights reserved © 1971 by United Feature Syndicate, Inc.
HERE I AM AGAIN...STILL LOOKING FOR THE ANSWERS!
SCHULZ
3-29

PEANUTS
THE ANSWER IS TWELVE!
IT ISN'T? HOW ABOUT SIX?
Tm. Reg. U.S. Pat. Off.—All rights reserved © 1971 by United Feature Syndicate, Inc.
FOUR? NINE? TWO? TEN?
4-30
DO YOU HAVE THE FEELING THAT I'M GUESSING?
SCHULZ

PEANUTS
SUMMER IS ALMOST OVER!
SCHOOL STARTS IN THREE WEEKS!!
8-18
PANIC IN THE STREETS!
Tm. Reg. U. S. Pat. Off.—All rights reserved
© 1971 by United Feature Syndicate, Inc.
PANIC IN THE STREETS?
SCHULZ

PEANUTS
Dear Grandma,
School starts again next week.
Tm. Reg. U. S. Pat. Off.—All rights reserved
© 1971 by United Feature Syndicate, Inc.
I hope I get my same desk on the I'll.
"I'LL"?
HAHAHAHAHAHA YAKYAKYAK!
THAT STUPID BEAGLE IS MAKING FUN OF MY LACK OF EDUCATION!
9-4
SCHULZ

PEANUTS
YOU'RE REALLY SOMETHING, DO YOU KNOW THAT?
I'VE NEVER SEEN ANYONE WHO WAS SO UPTIGHT ABOUT SCHOOL!
9-7
WHY DON'T YOU JUST RELAX?
WHO CAN RELAX?
SCHULZ
Tm. Reg. U. S. Pat. Off.—All rights reserved
© 1971 by United Feature Syndicate, Inc.

PEANUTS
I APPRECIATE IT! I APPRECIATE IT!
9-9
YES, I APPRECIATE IT! OH, YES, I REALLY APPRECIATE IT! I APPRECIATE IT!
I APPRECIATE IT!!!
Tm. Reg. U.S. Pat. Off.—All rights reserved © 1971 by United Feature Syndicate, Inc.
I LOVE "ART APPRECIATION"!
SCHULZ

PEANUTS
THIS IS AN ARTICLE I'VE WRITTEN FOR SCHOOL CALLED "WILD ANIMALS OF THE WEST"
"THERE ARE MANY WILD ANIMALS WHO LIVE IN THE WEST..SOME WHO LIVE IN THE MOUNTAINS ARE CALLED MOUNTAIN LIONS..."
"NOW, OF COURSE, WHERE YOU HAVE MOUNTAINS, YOU HAVE GULLIES... THE WILD ANIMALS WHO LIVE IN THE GULLIES ARE CALLED...."
10-20
"... GULLY CATS"?
Tm. Reg. U.S. Pat. Off.—All rights reserved © 1971 by United Feature Syndicate, Inc.
SCHULZ

PEANUTS
WE'RE GOING TO HAVE TO LEARN THE METRIC SYSTEM, FRANKLIN..
11-19
BY THE TIME WE GROW UP, THE METRIC SYSTEM WILL PROBABLY BE OFFICIAL..
ONE INCH IS 2.54 CENTIMETERS.. ONE FOOT IS 0.3048 METERS AND ONE MILE IS 1.609 KILOMETERS...
Tm. Reg. U.S. Pat. Off.—All rights reserved © 1971 by United Feature Syndicate, Inc.
I'LL NEVER MEASURE ANYTHING AGAIN AS LONG AS I LIVE!
SCHULZ

PEANUTS
HOW ABOUT A GAME OF MARBLES AFTER SCHOOL, FRANKLIN?
I CAN'T.. I HAVE A GUITAR LESSON AT THREE-THIRTY...
RIGHT AFTER THAT I HAVE LITTLE LEAGUE, AND THEN SWIM CLUB, AND THEN DINNER AND THEN A '4 H' MEETING
3-21
I LEAD A VERY ACTIVE TUESDAY!
Tm. Reg. U.S. Pat. Off.—All rights reserved © 1972 by United Feature Syndicate, Inc.
SCHULZ

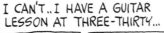

PEANUTS
STUDYING POETRY SPOILS THE POEMS
WHY DO WE HAVE TO TRY TO EXPLAIN A POEM?
THAT'S LIKE TRYING TO EXPLAIN A SUMMER SKY, OR A WINTER MOON...
4-26
Tm. Reg. U.S. Pat. Off.—All rights reserved © 1972 by United Feature Syndicate, Inc.
..OR A PRETTY FACE!
SCHULZ

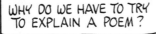

PEANUTS
I LEARNED TWO THINGS IN SCHOOL TODAY
I LEARNED THAT IF YOU DON'T WATCH WHERE YOU'RE GOING, YOU CAN GET KNOCKED DOWN IN THE HALL...
AND I ALSO LEARNED THAT THE DRINKING FOUNTAIN IS OUT OF ORDER!
5-2
Tm. Reg. U.S. Pat. Off.—All rights reserved © 1972 by United Feature Syndicate, Inc.
IT'S NOT OFTEN THAT YOU CAN LEARN TWO NEW THINGS IN ONE DAY!
SCHULZ

PEANUTS
WHO WAS THE FATHER OF HENRY IV ?
I COULD NOT POSSIBLY CARE LESS!
5-5
I'M SORRY... I APOLOGIZE..
Tm. Reg. U.S. Pat. Off.—All rights reserved © 1972 by United Feature Syndicate, Inc.
THAT WAS JUST A GUT REACTION
SCHULZ

PEANUTS
8-30
Tm. Reg. U.S. Pat. Off.—All rights reserved © 1972 by United Feature Syndicate, Inc.
SCHOOL STARTS AGAIN NEXT WEEK...
I THINK I'VE RUINED HER EYES FOR GOOD!
SCHULZ

PEANUTS
YES, MA'AM...WE'D LIKE TO BORROW THE LATEST BOOK BY MISS HELEN SWEETSTORY..
Tm. Reg. U.S. Pat. Off.—All rights reserved © 1972 by United Feature Syndicate, Inc.
BANNED?!!
IT'S BEEN BANNED FROM THE SCHOOL LIBRARY! I CAN'T BELIEVE IT!
10-23
HOW COULD ANYONE BAN SUCH A NEAT BOOK AS "THE SIX BUNNY-WUNNIES FREAK OUT"?
SCHULZ

PEANUTS
WHY WOULD THEY BAN MISS SWEETSTORY'S BOOK FROM THE SCHOOL LIBRARY?
I CAN'T BELIEVE IT.. I JUST CAN'T BELIEVE IT!
MAYBE THERE ARE SOME THINGS IN HER BOOK THAT WE DON'T UNDERSTAND...
IN THAT CASE, THEY SHOULD ALSO BAN MY MATH BOOK!
Tm. Reg. U. S. Pat. Off.—All rights reserved © 1972 by United Feature Syndicate, Inc.

PEANUTS
Tm. Reg. U. S. Pat. Off.—All rights reserved © 1972 by United Feature Syndicate, Inc.
I'M AWAKE!!

PEANUTS
Tm. Reg. U. S. Pat. Off.—All rights reserved © 1972 by United Feature Syndicate, Inc.
BETTY? YES, MA'AM.. I ADMIT IT...
I SIGNED MY ENGLISH REPORT "BETTY"
IT WASN'T MUCH OF A REPORT...
I CHANGED MY NAME TO PROTECT THE INNOCENT

PEANUTS
THIS IS SOME TEST
"WHO WAS CYRIL FOX? DISCUSS BRIEFLY THE BRONZE AGE"
"WHO WERE THE BEAKER PEOPLE? WHO WAS CASSIVELLAUNUS? WHO WAS CUNOBELIN? WHAT WERE THE CAUSEWAYED CAMPS?"
Tm. Reg. U.S. Pat. Off.—All rights reserved © 1973 by United Feature Syndicate, Inc.
1-17
IT'S GUESSING TIME!
SCHULZ

PEANUTS
SCHOOL STARTS IN TWO WEEKS...
I THOUGHT I HAD ALREADY LEARNED EVERYTHING THERE WAS TO KNOW...
HARDLY
8-24
IS IT POSSIBLE FOR ME TO LEARN EVERYTHING THERE IS TO KNOW?
HARDLY
HOW COME I ALWAYS GET CAUGHT IN THE MIDDLE?
SCHULZ

PEANUTS
I HAVE A QUESTION...
WHEN I START SCHOOL NEXT WEEK, WILL I GET THE SAME DESK I HAD LAST YEAR?
8-28
PROBABLY NOT
HOW WILL I KNOW THAT MY NEW DESK HASN'T BEEN BUGGED?
SCHULZ

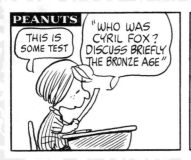

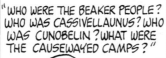

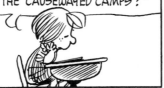

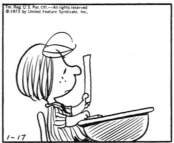

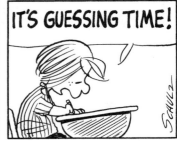

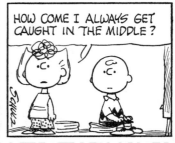

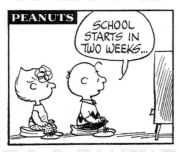

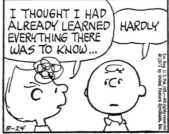

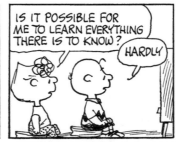

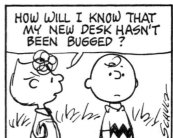

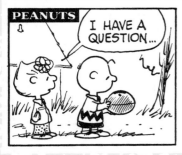

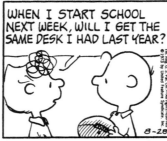

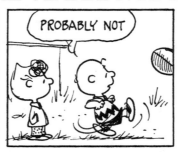

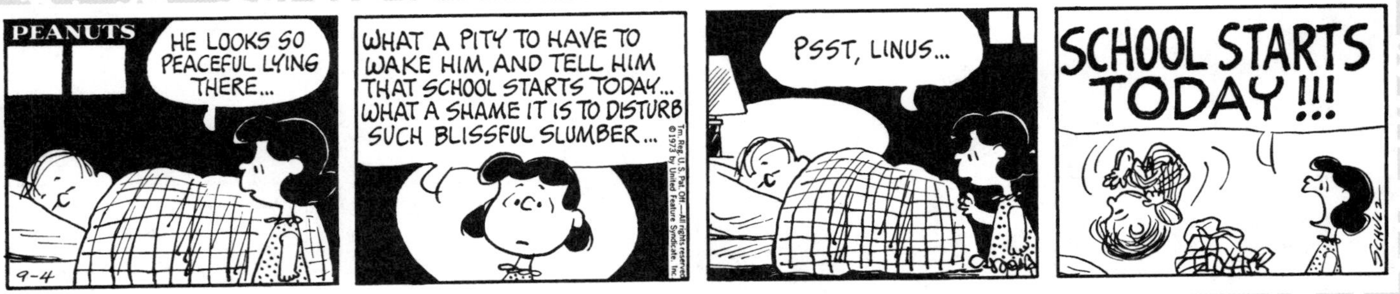
PEANUTS
HE LOOKS SO PEACEFUL LYING THERE...
9-4
WHAT A PITY TO HAVE TO WAKE HIM, AND TELL HIM THAT SCHOOL STARTS TODAY... WHAT A SHAME IT IS TO DISTURB SUCH BLISSFUL SLUMBER...
Tm. Reg. U.S. Pat. Off.—All rights reserved © 1973 by United Feature Syndicate, Inc.
PSST, LINUS...
SCHOOL STARTS TODAY!!!
SCHULZ

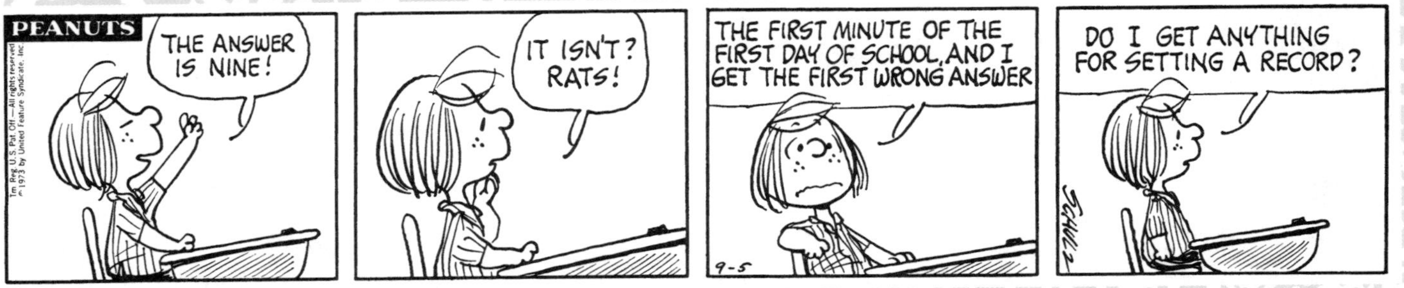
PEANUTS
Tm. Reg. U.S. Pat. Off.—All rights reserved © 1973 by United Feature Syndicate, Inc.
THE ANSWER IS NINE!
IT ISN'T? RATS!
THE FIRST MINUTE OF THE FIRST DAY OF SCHOOL, AND I GET THE FIRST WRONG ANSWER
9-5
DO I GET ANYTHING FOR SETTING A RECORD?
SCHULZ

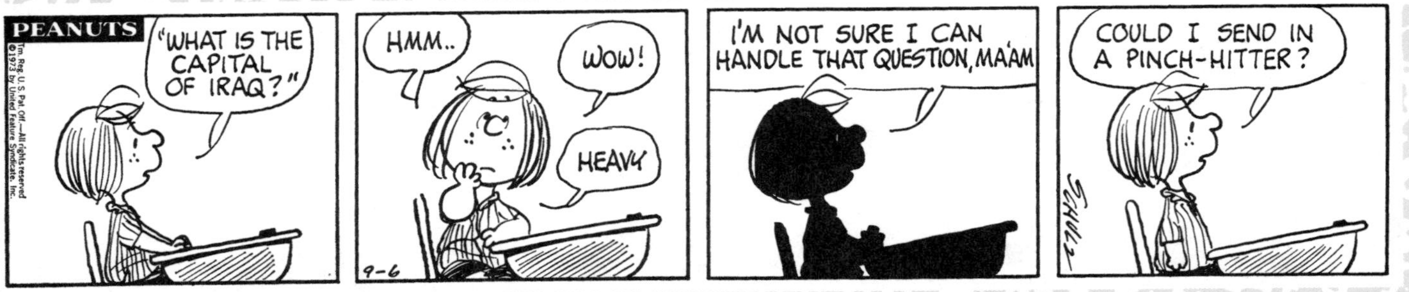
PEANUTS
Tm. Reg. U.S. Pat. Off.—All rights reserved © 1973 by United Feature Syndicate, Inc.
"WHAT IS THE CAPITAL OF IRAQ?"
HMM..
WOW!
HEAVY
9-6
I'M NOT SURE I CAN HANDLE THAT QUESTION, MA'AM
COULD I SEND IN A PINCH-HITTER?
SCHULZ

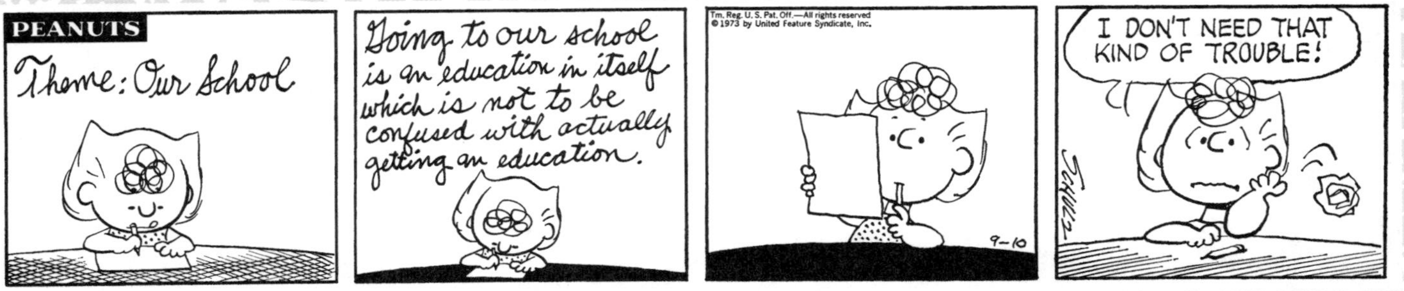
PEANUTS
Theme: Our School
Going to our school is an education in itself which is not to be confused with actually getting an education.
Tm. Reg. U.S. Pat. Off.—All rights reserved © 1973 by United Feature Syndicate, Inc.
9-10
I DON'T NEED THAT KIND OF TROUBLE!
SCHULZ

PEANUTS
TRUE! FALSE! TRUE!
9-12
TRUE! FALSE! FALSE! TRUE! FALSE! FALSE! TRUE! FALSE!
Tm. Reg. U.S. Pat. Off.—All rights reserved © 1973 by United Feature Syndicate, Inc.
TRUE! FALSE! TRUE! TRUE! FALSE! TRUE! TRUE! TRUE! TRUE! FALSE! TRUE! FALSE!
AND ONE GOOD OLD FASHIONED MAYBE!!
SCHULZ

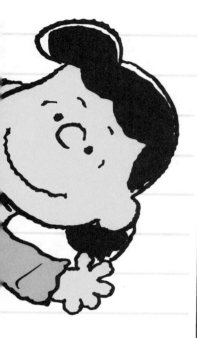

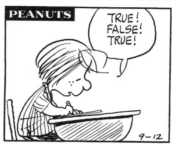

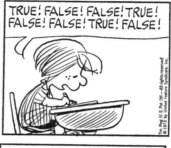

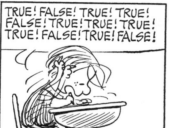

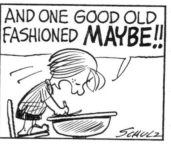

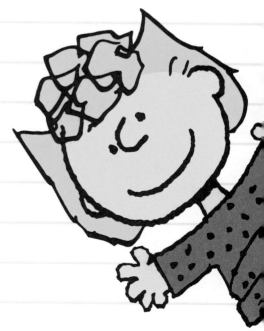

PEANUTS
WELL, HERE I AM AGAIN... THE ANXIOUS PUPIL!
9-20
READY TO LEARN... READY TO ABSORB...
Tm. Reg. U.S. Pat. Off.—All rights reserved © 1973 by United Feature Syndicate, Inc.
EDUCATE ME IN THE WORLD'S WAYS! MAKE OF ME A VESSEL FOR THY TEACHING!
LET'S LEARN THOSE CAPITALS!!
SCHULZ

PEANUTS
Tm. Reg. U.S. Pat. Off.—All rights reserved © 1973 by United Feature Syndicate, Inc.
This is my report on rain. Rain is water which does not come out of faucets.
If it were not for rain, we would not get wet walking to school and get a sore throat and stay home which is not a bad idea.
11-7
Rain was the inspiration for that immortal poem, "Rain, rain, go away. Come again some other day."
After a storm, the rain goes down the drain which is where I sometimes feel my education is also going. End of report
SCHULZ

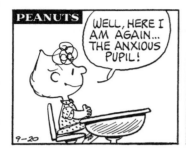

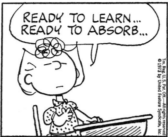

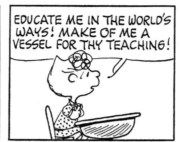

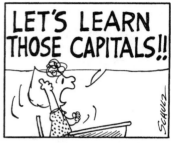

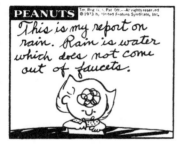

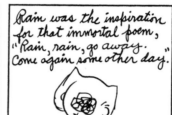

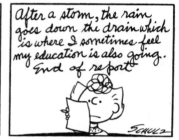

PEANUTS KING LOUIS THE SECOND?

WELL, IF YOU SUBTRACT KING LOUIS THE FOURTEENTH FROM KING LOUIS THE SIXTEENTH, YOU GET KING LOUIS THE SECOND!

YOU DON'T?

RATS! I THOUGHT THAT WAS A PRETTY GOOD ANSWER!

PEANUTS I OBJECT!!

I WANT TO KNOW WHY I RECEIVED SUCH A TERRIBLE GRADE ON MY PAPER...

I SEE

NO FURTHER QUESTIONS, YOUR HONOR!

PEANUTS

YES, MA'AM... I'M BACK FROM THE PRINCIPAL'S OFFICE...

HE SAID I SHOULD TRY HARDER AT PAYING ATTENTION...

HOW'S THIS?

FORGET IT! THAT PAYING ATTENTION COULD KILL YOU!

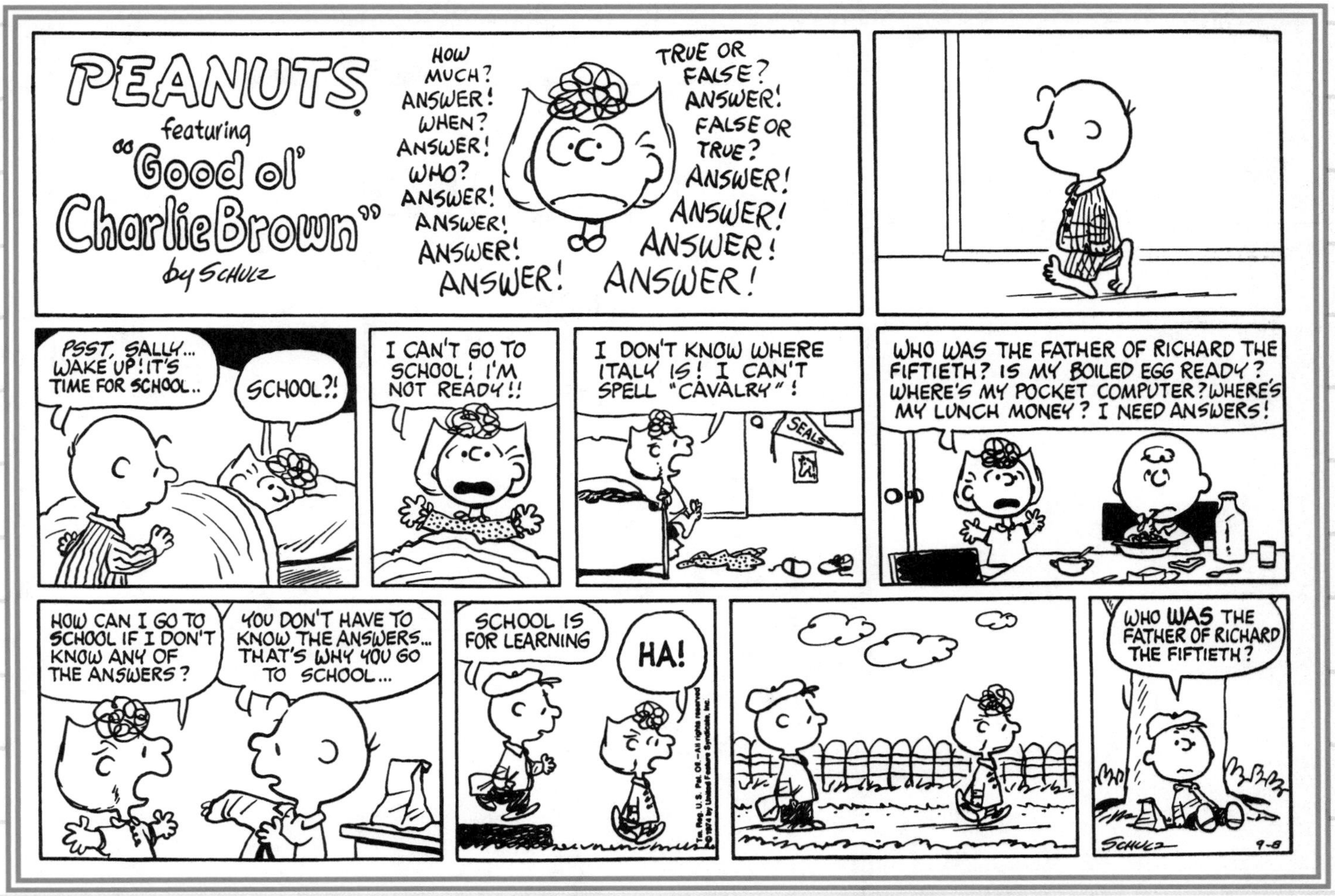
PEANUTS featuring "Good ol' Charlie Brown" by SCHULZ
HOW MUCH? ANSWER! WHEN? ANSWER! WHO? ANSWER! ANSWER! ANSWER! ANSWER!
TRUE OR FALSE? ANSWER! FALSE OR TRUE? ANSWER! ANSWER! ANSWER! ANSWER!
PSST, SALLY... WAKE UP! IT'S TIME FOR SCHOOL..
SCHOOL?!
I CAN'T GO TO SCHOOL! I'M NOT READY!!
I DON'T KNOW WHERE ITALY IS! I CAN'T SPELL "CAVALRY"!
SEALS
WHO WAS THE FATHER OF RICHARD THE FIFTIETH? IS MY BOILED EGG READY? WHERE'S MY POCKET COMPUTER? WHERE'S MY LUNCH MONEY? I NEED ANSWERS!
HOW CAN I GO TO SCHOOL IF I DON'T KNOW ANY OF THE ANSWERS?
YOU DON'T HAVE TO KNOW THE ANSWERS... THAT'S WHY YOU GO TO SCHOOL...
SCHOOL IS FOR LEARNING
HA!
WHO WAS THE FATHER OF RICHARD THE FIFTIETH?
SCHULZ 9-8

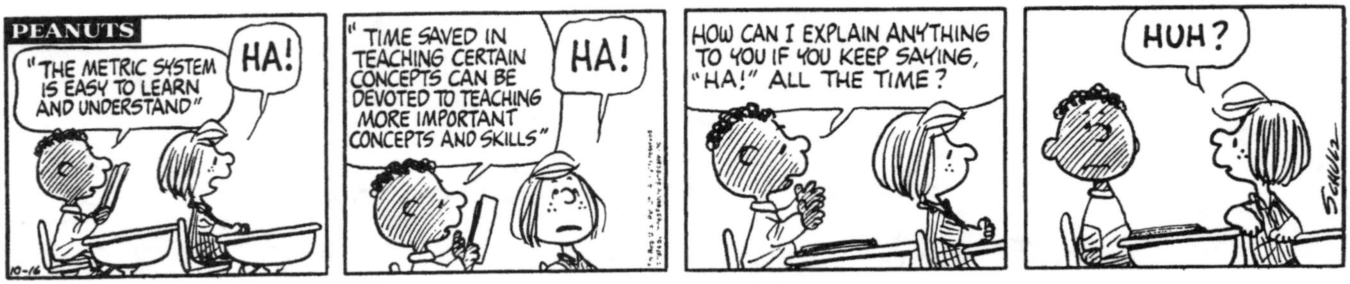
PEANUTS
"THE METRIC SYSTEM IS EASY TO LEARN AND UNDERSTAND"
HA!
"TIME SAVED IN TEACHING CERTAIN CONCEPTS CAN BE DEVOTED TO TEACHING MORE IMPORTANT CONCEPTS AND SKILLS"
HA!
HOW CAN I EXPLAIN ANYTHING TO YOU IF YOU KEEP SAYING, "HA!" ALL THE TIME?
HUH?
10-16
SCHULZ

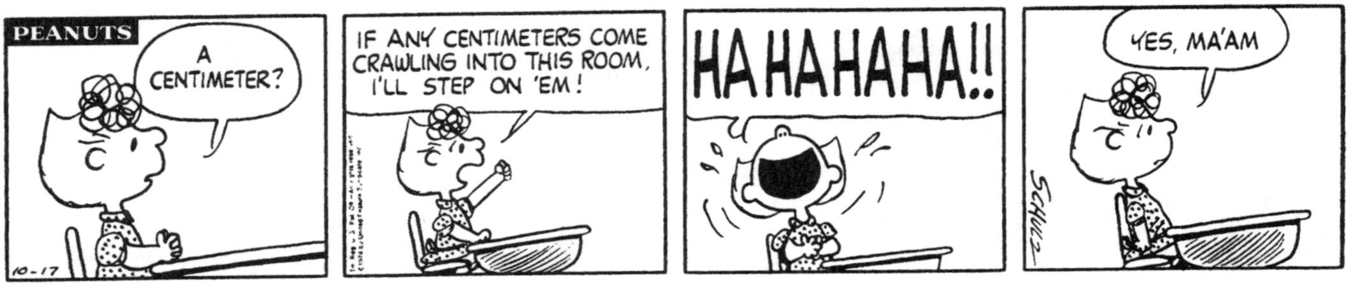
PEANUTS
A CENTIMETER?
IF ANY CENTIMETERS COME CRAWLING INTO THIS ROOM, I'LL STEP ON 'EM!
HAHAHAHA!!
YES, MA'AM
10-17
SCHULZ

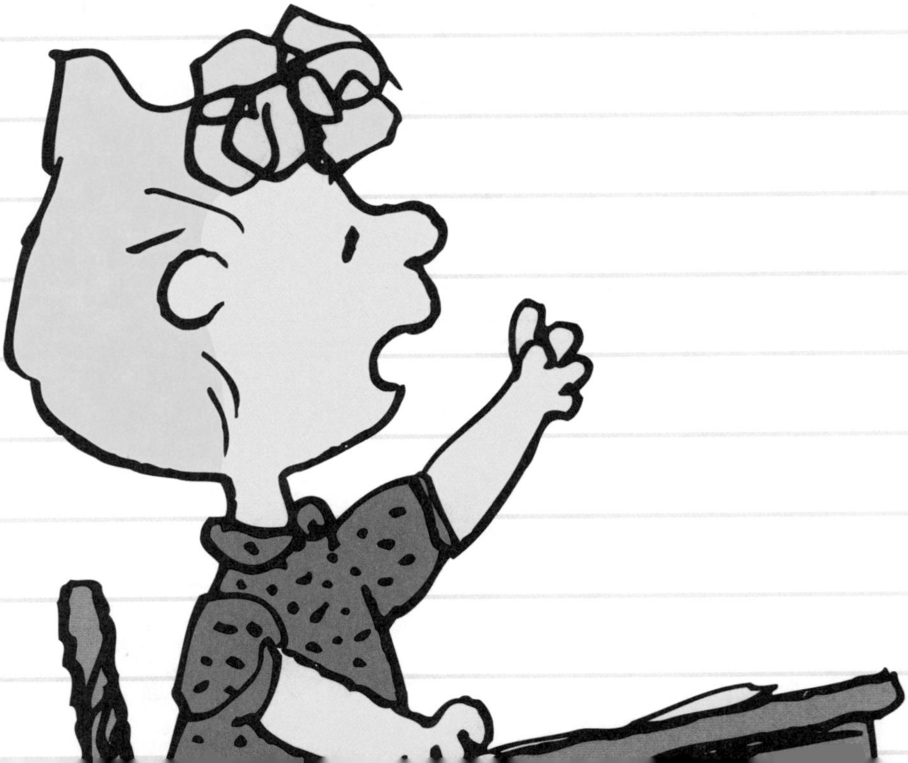

PEANUTS
"THINK METRIC"... PASS IT ON!
"THINK METRIC!" PASS IT ON!
Tm. Reg. U. S. Pat. Off.—All rights reserved
©1974 by United Feature Syndicate, Inc.
"THINK METRIC!" PASS IT ON!
AAUGHH!
SCHULZ
10-18

PEANUTS
"HOW MANY BARRELS IN A HOGSHEAD?"
Tm Reg U S. Pat. Off —All rights reserved
©1974 by United Feature Syndicate, Inc.
"HOW MANY INCHES IN A NAIL? HOW MANY NAILS IN A QUARTER? HOW MANY SQUARE RODS IN A ROOD?"
HOW MANY WHATS IN A WHO? HOW MANY WHOS IN A WHAT?!
SCHULZ
IT'S ZERO TIME!
10-25

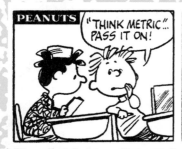

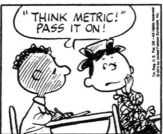

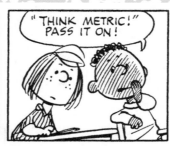

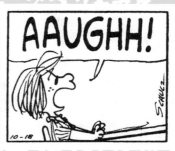

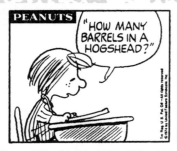

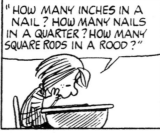

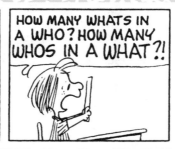

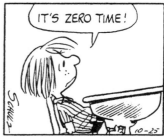

PEANUTS
FACTOR $\frac{1}{36}x^2-9y^4$
10-29
GOOD GRIEF!!
$\frac{1}{36}x^2-9y^4=\left(\frac{1}{6}x\right)^2-(3y^2)^2$
$=\left(\frac{1}{6}x-3y^2\right)\left(\frac{1}{6}x+3y^2\right)$
OVER THE YEARS I'VE LEARNED A FEW THINGS
SCHULZ
Tm. Reg. U. S. Pat. Off.—All rights reserved
©1974 by United Feature Syndicate, Inc.

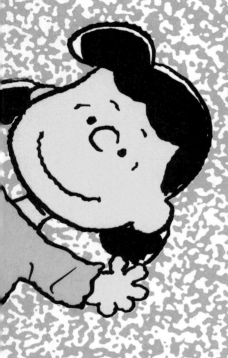

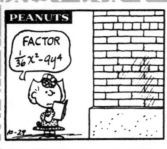

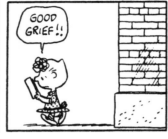

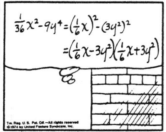

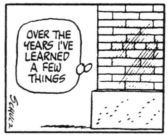

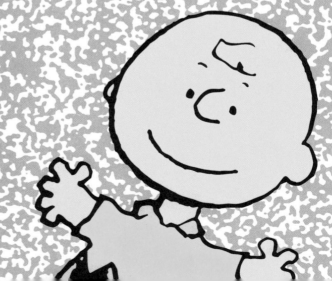

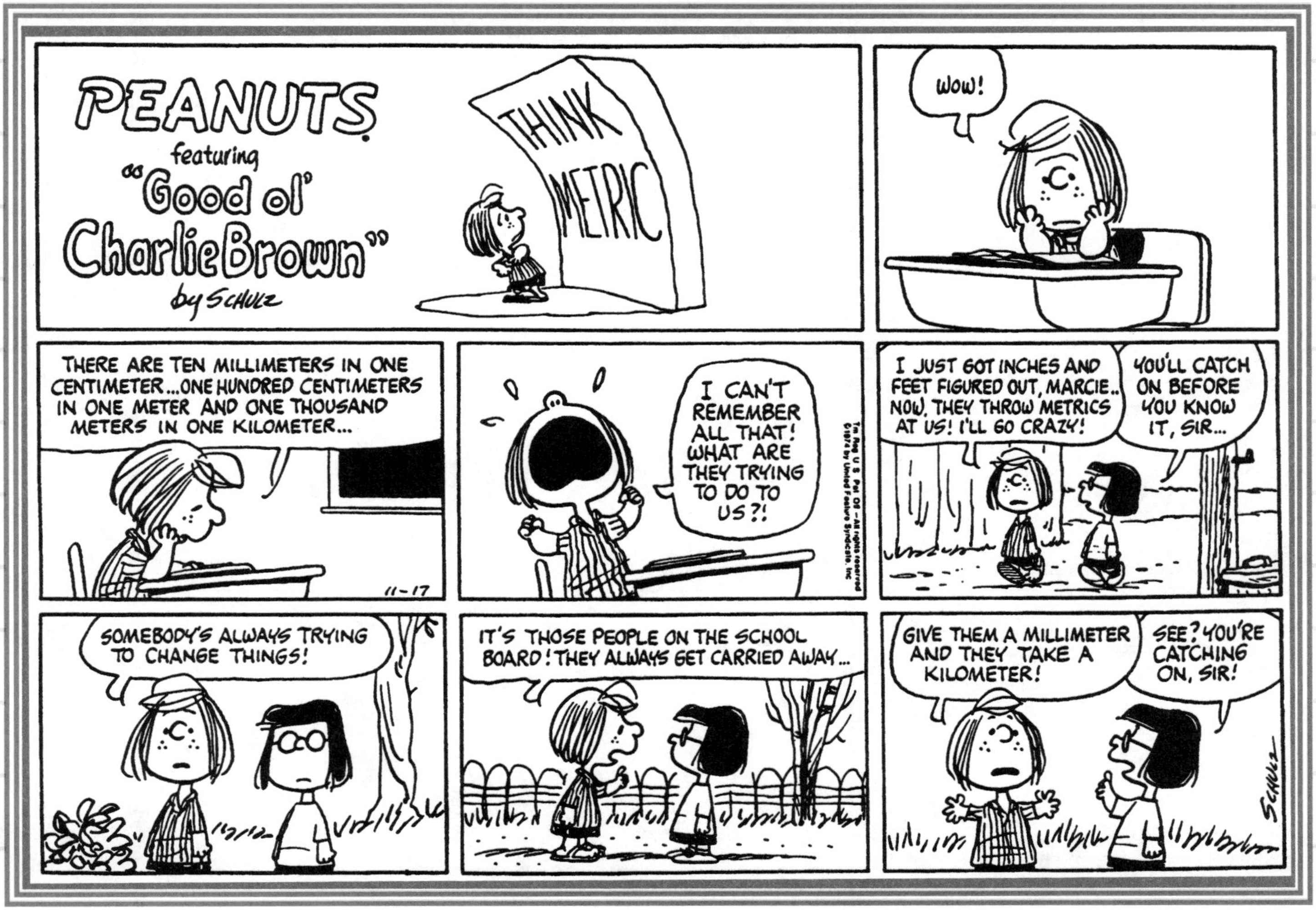
PEANUTS
featuring
"Good ol' CharlieBrown"
by SCHULZ
THINK METRIC
WOW!
THERE ARE TEN MILLIMETERS IN ONE CENTIMETER...ONE HUNDRED CENTIMETERS IN ONE METER AND ONE THOUSAND METERS IN ONE KILOMETER...
11-17
I CAN'T REMEMBER ALL THAT! WHAT ARE THEY TRYING TO DO TO US?!
Tm Reg U S Pat Off—All rights reserved ©1974 by United Feature Syndicate, Inc.
I JUST GOT INCHES AND FEET FIGURED OUT, MARCIE.. NOW, THEY THROW METRICS AT US! I'LL GO CRAZY!
YOU'LL CATCH ON BEFORE YOU KNOW IT, SIR...
SOMEBODY'S ALWAYS TRYING TO CHANGE THINGS!
IT'S THOSE PEOPLE ON THE SCHOOL BOARD! THEY ALWAYS GET CARRIED AWAY...
GIVE THEM A MILLIMETER AND THEY TAKE A KILOMETER!
SEE? YOU'RE CATCHING ON, SIR!
SCHULZ

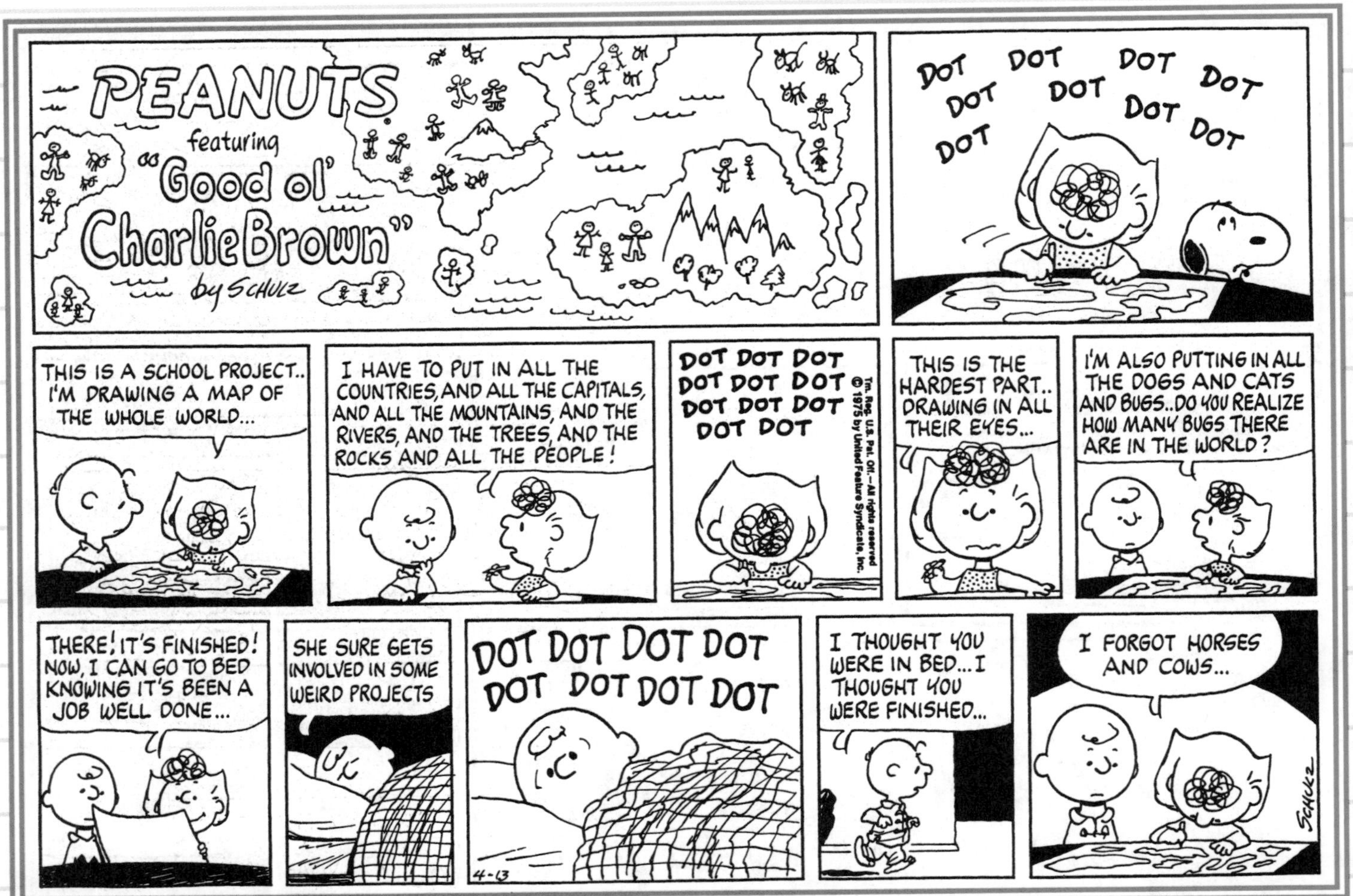
PEANUTS
featuring "Good ol' Charlie Brown"
by SCHULZ
DOT DOT DOT DOT DOT DOT DOT DOT DOT
THIS IS A SCHOOL PROJECT.. I'M DRAWING A MAP OF THE WHOLE WORLD...
I HAVE TO PUT IN ALL THE COUNTRIES, AND ALL THE CAPITALS, AND ALL THE MOUNTAINS, AND THE RIVERS, AND THE TREES, AND THE ROCKS AND ALL THE PEOPLE!
DOT DOT DOT DOT DOT DOT DOT DOT DOT DOT DOT
Tm. Reg. U.S. Pat. Off.—All rights reserved © 1975 by United Feature Syndicate, Inc.
THIS IS THE HARDEST PART.. DRAWING IN ALL THEIR EYES...
I'M ALSO PUTTING IN ALL THE DOGS AND CATS AND BUGS..DO YOU REALIZE HOW MANY BUGS THERE ARE IN THE WORLD?
THERE! IT'S FINISHED! NOW, I CAN GO TO BED KNOWING IT'S BEEN A JOB WELL DONE...
SHE SURE GETS INVOLVED IN SOME WEIRD PROJECTS
DOT DOT DOT DOT DOT DOT DOT DOT
4-13
I THOUGHT YOU WERE IN BED... I THOUGHT YOU WERE FINISHED...
I FORGOT HORSES AND COWS...
SCHULZ

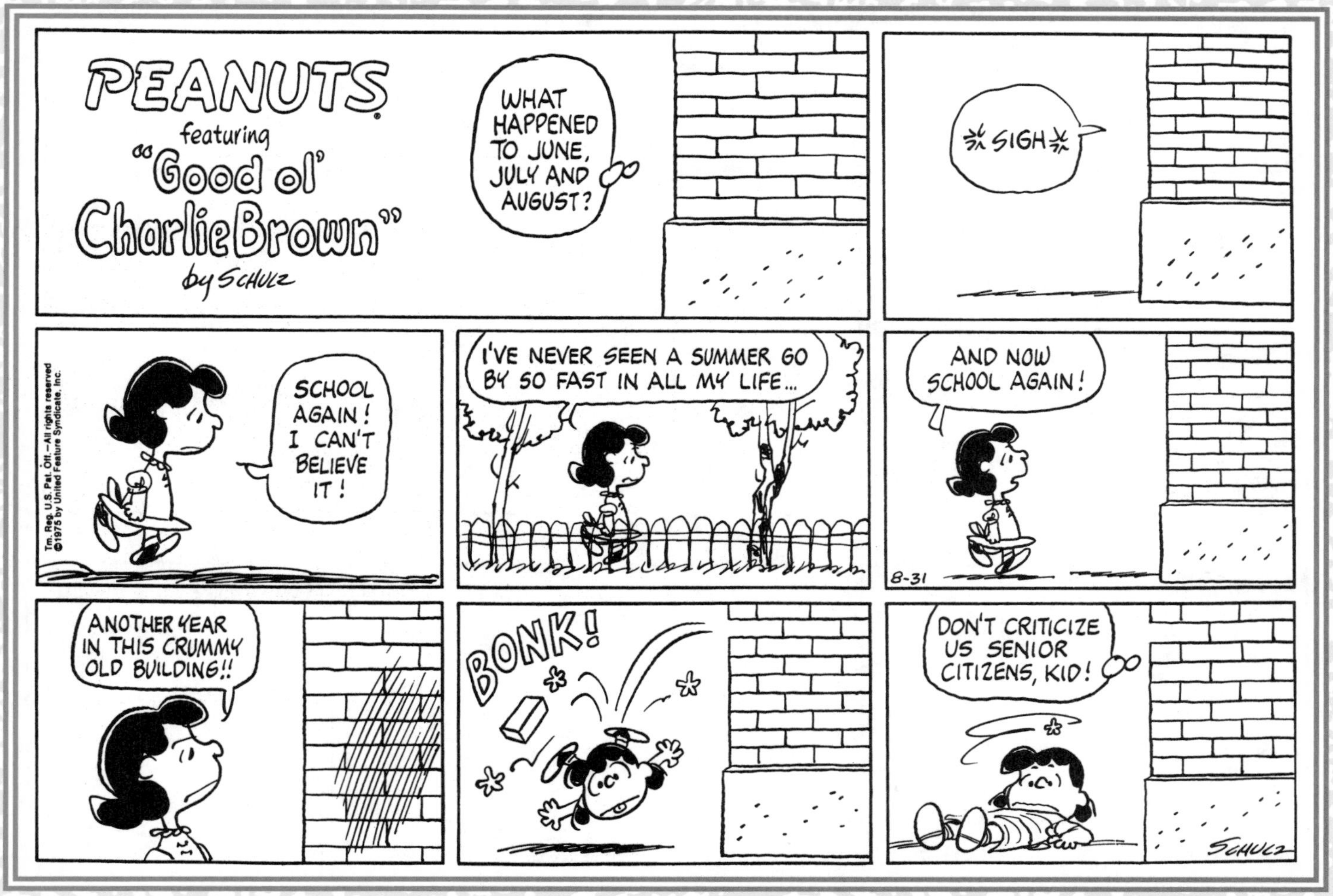
PEANUTS
featuring
"Good ol' Charlie Brown"
by SCHULZ
WHAT HAPPENED TO JUNE, JULY AND AUGUST?
SIGH
Tm. Reg. U.S. Pat. Off.—All rights reserved
©1975 by United Feature Syndicate, Inc.
SCHOOL AGAIN! I CAN'T BELIEVE IT!
I'VE NEVER SEEN A SUMMER GO BY SO FAST IN ALL MY LIFE...
AND NOW SCHOOL AGAIN!
8-31
ANOTHER YEAR IN THIS CRUMMY OLD BUILDING!!
BONK!
DON'T CRITICIZE US SENIOR CITIZENS, KID!
SCHULZ

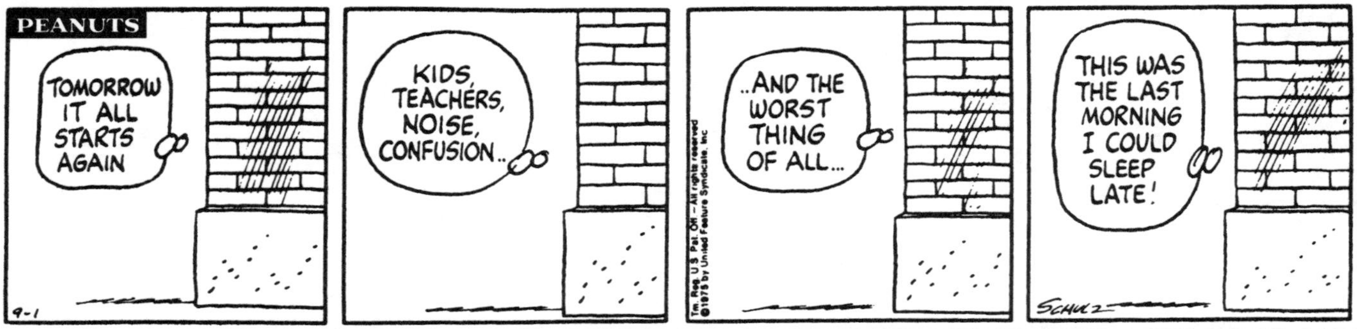
PEANUTS
TOMORROW IT ALL STARTS AGAIN
KIDS, TEACHERS, NOISE, CONFUSION..
..AND THE WORST THING OF ALL...
THIS WAS THE LAST MORNING I COULD SLEEP LATE!
9-1
Tm. Reg. U.S. Pat. Off.—All rights reserved ©1975 by United Feature Syndicate, Inc.
SCHULZ

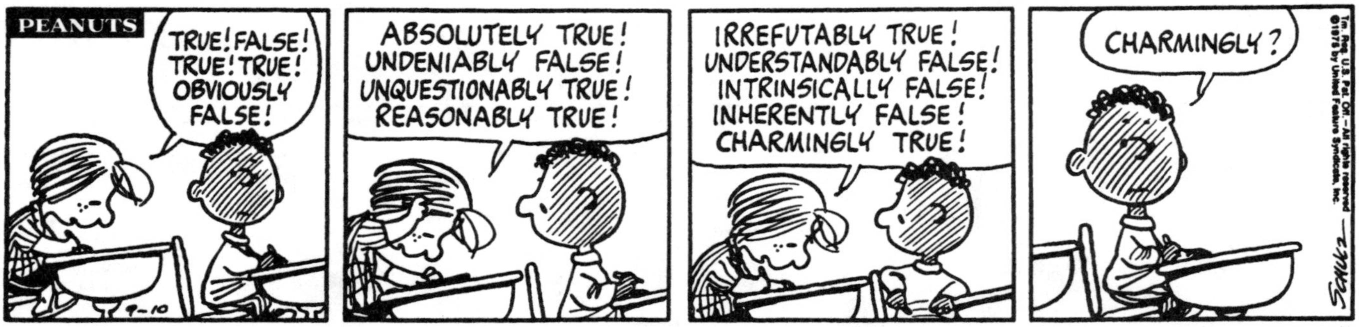
PEANUTS
TRUE! FALSE! TRUE! TRUE! OBVIOUSLY FALSE!
ABSOLUTELY TRUE! UNDENIABLY FALSE! UNQUESTIONABLY TRUE! REASONABLY TRUE!
IRREFUTABLY TRUE! UNDERSTANDABLY FALSE! INTRINSICALLY FALSE! INHERENTLY FALSE! CHARMINGLY TRUE!
CHARMINGLY?
9-10
Tm. Reg. U.S. Pat. Off.—All rights reserved ©1975 by United Feature Syndicate, Inc.
SCHULZ

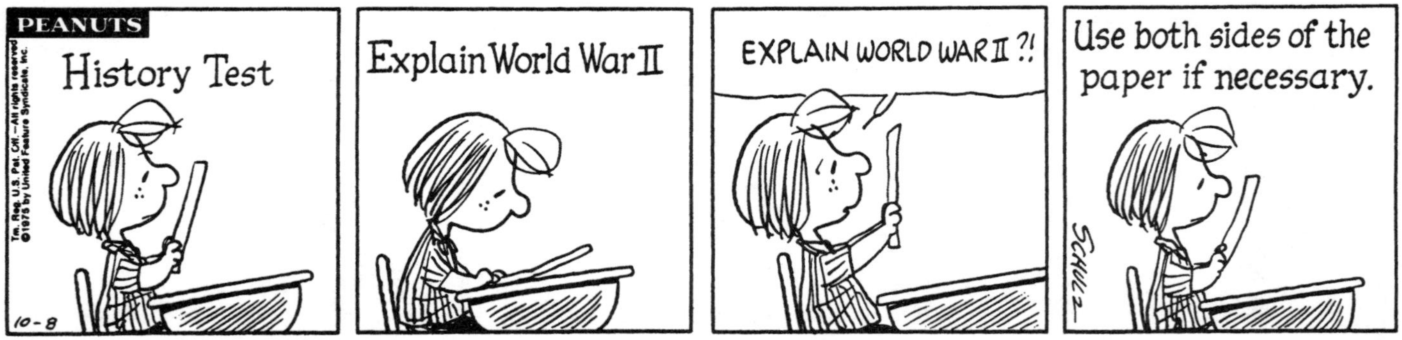
PEANUTS
History Test
Explain World War II
EXPLAIN WORLD WAR II ?!
Use both sides of the paper if necessary.
10-8
Tm. Reg. U.S. Pat. Off.—All rights reserved ©1975 by United Feature Syndicate, Inc.
SCHULZ

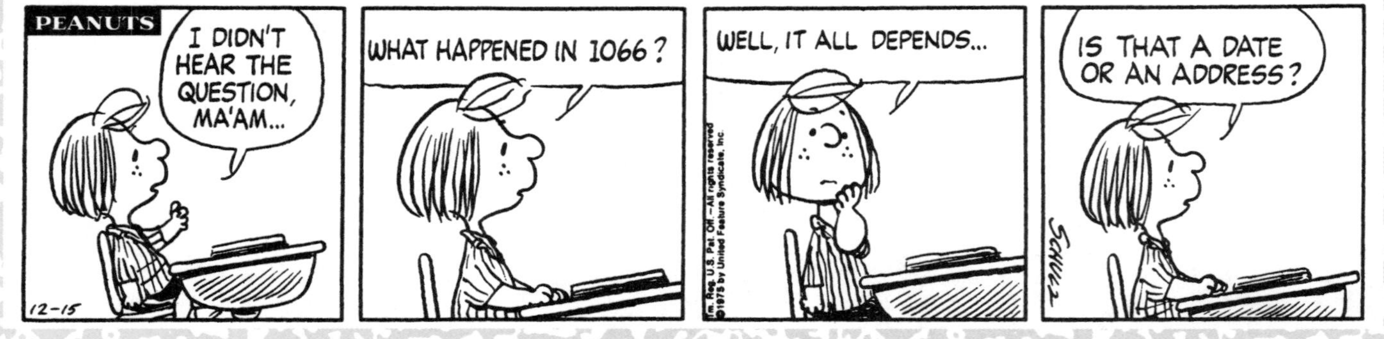
PEANUTS
I DIDN'T HEAR THE QUESTION, MA'AM...
WHAT HAPPENED IN 1066?
WELL, IT ALL DEPENDS...
IS THAT A DATE OR AN ADDRESS?
12-15
Tm. Reg. U.S. Pat. Off.—All rights reserved ©1975 by United Feature Syndicate, Inc.
SCHULZ

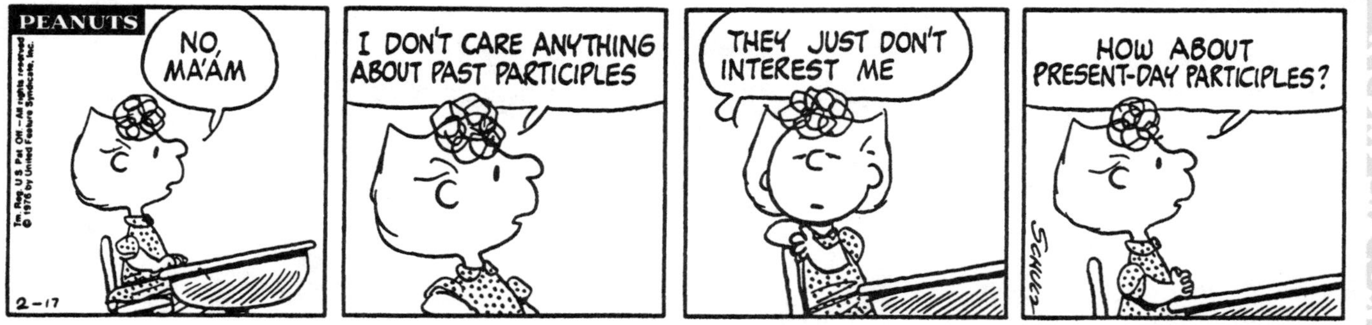
PEANUTS
Tm. Reg. U.S. Pat. Off.—All rights reserved © 1976 by United Feature Syndicate, Inc.
NO, MA'AM
2-17
I DON'T CARE ANYTHING ABOUT PAST PARTICIPLES
THEY JUST DON'T INTEREST ME
HOW ABOUT PRESENT-DAY PARTICIPLES?
SCHULZ

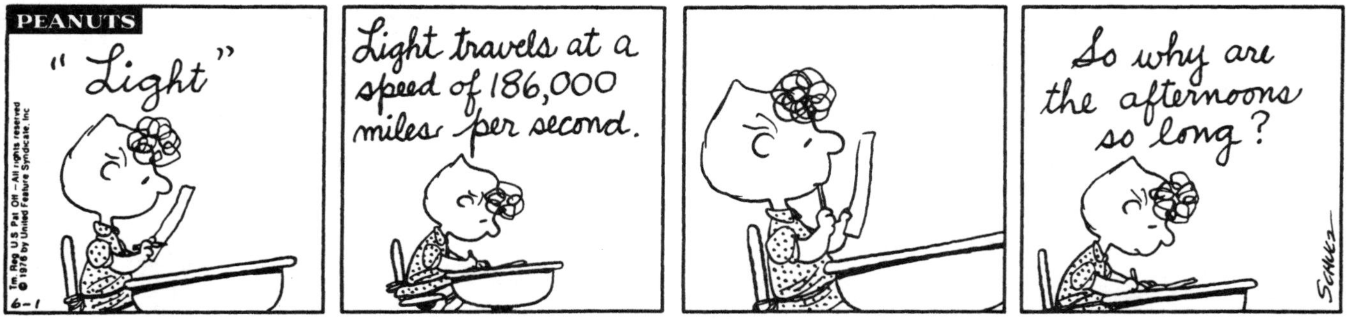
PEANUTS
Tm. Reg. U.S. Pat. Off.—All rights reserved © 1976 by United Feature Syndicate, Inc.
"Light"
6-1
Light travels at a speed of 186,000 miles per second.
So why are the afternoons so long?
SCHULZ

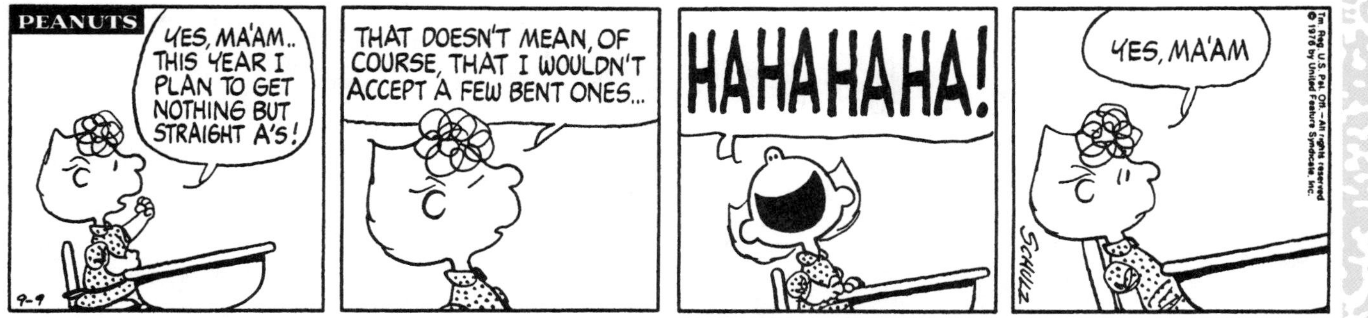
PEANUTS
YES, MA'AM.. THIS YEAR I PLAN TO GET NOTHING BUT STRAIGHT A'S!
9-9
THAT DOESN'T MEAN, OF COURSE, THAT I WOULDN'T ACCEPT A FEW BENT ONES...
HAHAHAHA!
YES, MA'AM
SCHULZ
Tm. Reg. U.S. Pat. Off.—All rights reserved © 1976 by United Feature Syndicate, Inc.

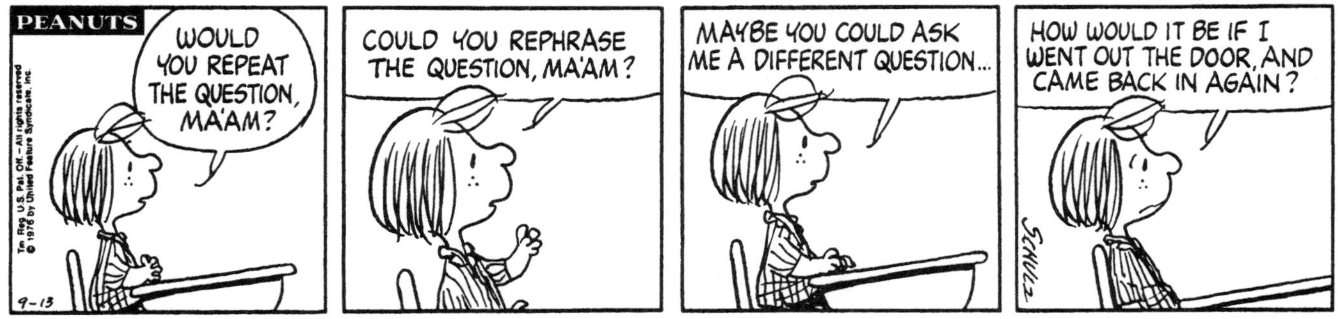
PEANUTS
Tm. Reg. U.S. Pat. Off.—All rights reserved © 1976 by United Feature Syndicate, Inc.
WOULD YOU REPEAT THE QUESTION, MA'AM?
9-13
COULD YOU REPHRASE THE QUESTION, MA'AM?
MAYBE YOU COULD ASK ME A DIFFERENT QUESTION...
HOW WOULD IT BE IF I WENT OUT THE DOOR, AND CAME BACK IN AGAIN?
SCHULZ

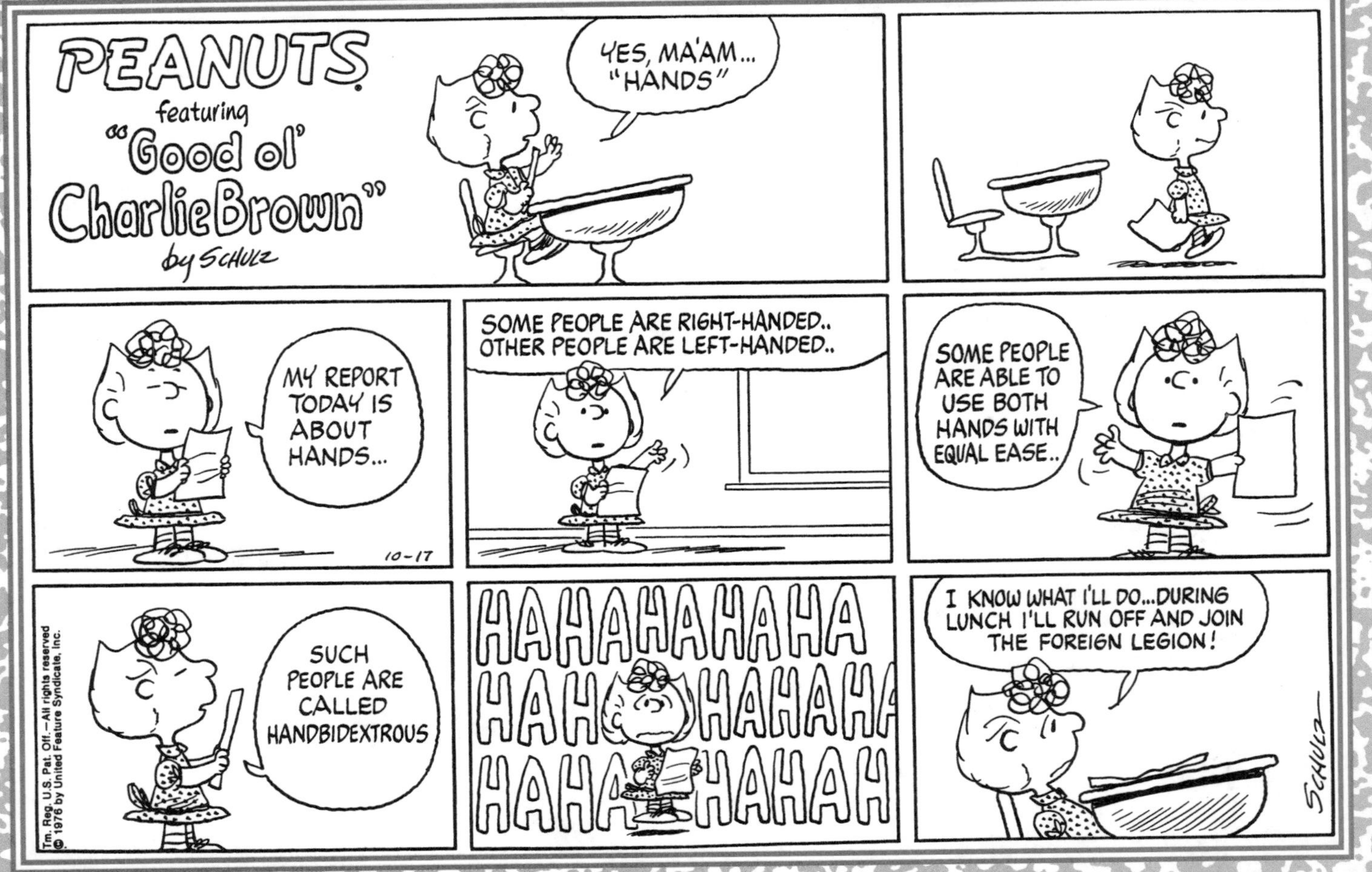
PEANUTS
featuring
"Good ol' CharlieBrown"
by SCHULZ
YES, MA'AM... "HANDS"
MY REPORT TODAY IS ABOUT HANDS...
10-17
SOME PEOPLE ARE RIGHT-HANDED.. OTHER PEOPLE ARE LEFT-HANDED..
SOME PEOPLE ARE ABLE TO USE BOTH HANDS WITH EQUAL EASE..
Tm. Reg. U.S. Pat. Off.—All rights reserved
© 1976 by United Feature Syndicate, Inc.
SUCH PEOPLE ARE CALLED HANDBIDEXTROUS
HAHAHAHAHAHA
HAHAHAHAHA
HAHAHAHAH
I KNOW WHAT I'LL DO...DURING LUNCH I'LL RUN OFF AND JOIN THE FOREIGN LEGION!
SCHULZ

PEANUTS
COULD YOU REPEAT THE QUESTION, MA'AM?
2-17
Tm. Reg. U.S. Pat. Off.—All rights reserved © 1977 by United Feature Syndicate, Inc.
YES, MA'AM... I UNDERSTAND..
"WHAT WAS THE AUTHOR'S PURPOSE IN WRITING THIS STORY?"
MAYBE HE NEEDED THE MONEY!
SCHULZ

YES, MA'AM..
4-11
MY REPORT IS READY
ONE QUESTION...
DO YOU WISH ME TO VERBALIZE OR ORALIZE?
SCHULZ
© 1977 United Feature Syndicate, Inc.

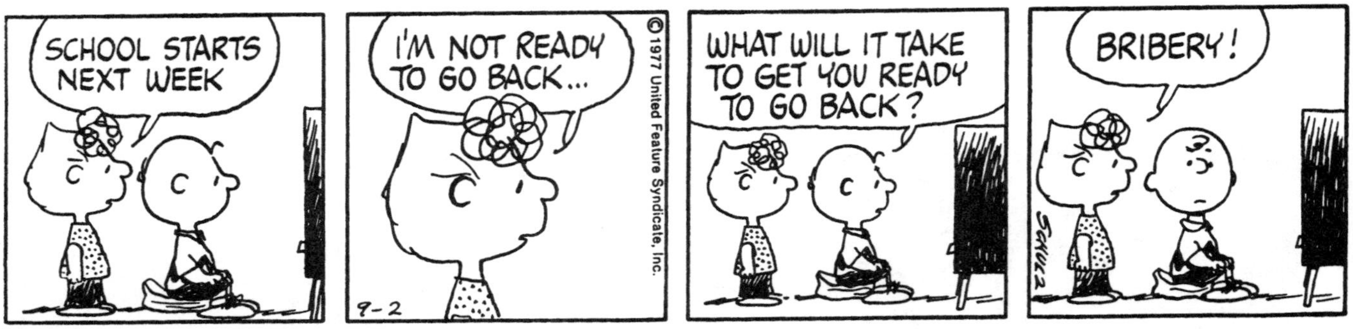
SCHOOL STARTS NEXT WEEK
I'M NOT READY TO GO BACK...
© 1977 United Feature Syndicate, Inc.
WHAT WILL IT TAKE TO GET YOU READY TO GO BACK?
BRIBERY!

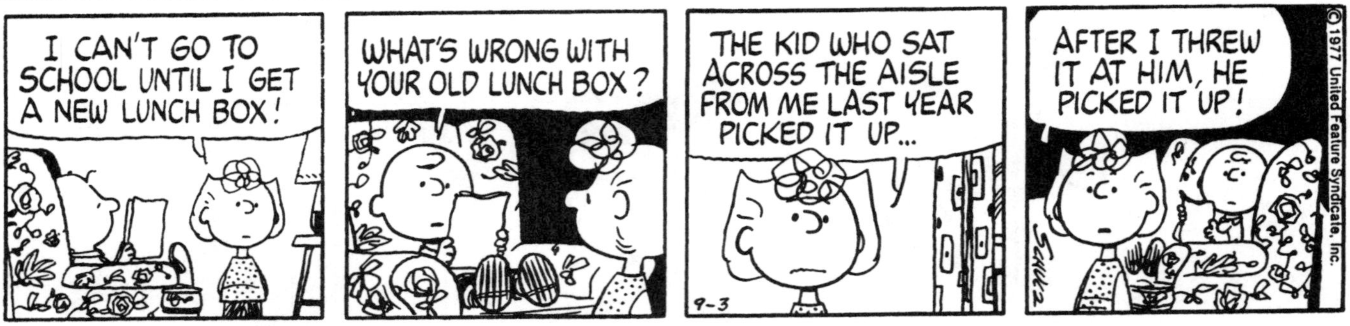
I CAN'T GO TO SCHOOL UNTIL I GET A NEW LUNCH BOX!
WHAT'S WRONG WITH YOUR OLD LUNCH BOX?
THE KID WHO SAT ACROSS THE AISLE FROM ME LAST YEAR PICKED IT UP...
AFTER I THREW IT AT HIM, HE PICKED IT UP!
© 1977 United Feature Syndicate, Inc.

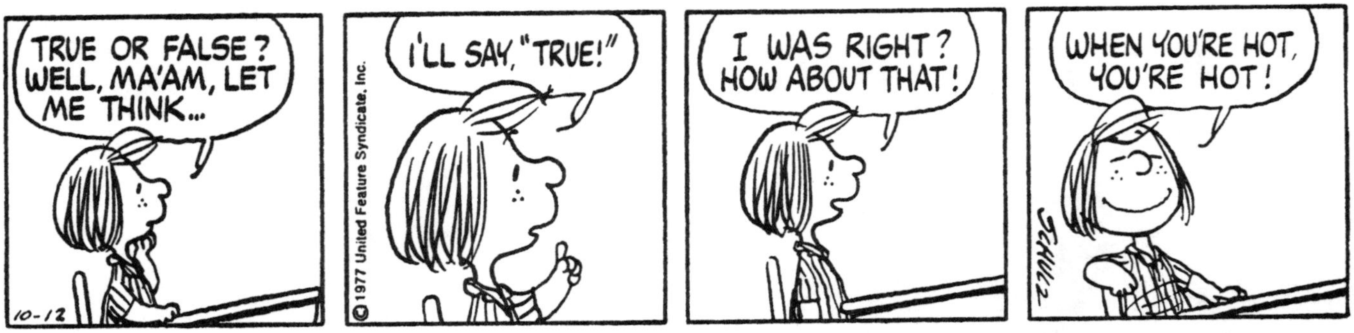
TRUE OR FALSE? WELL, MA'AM, LET ME THINK...
© 1977 United Feature Syndicate, Inc.
I'LL SAY, "TRUE!"
I WAS RIGHT? HOW ABOUT THAT!
WHEN YOU'RE HOT, YOU'RE HOT!

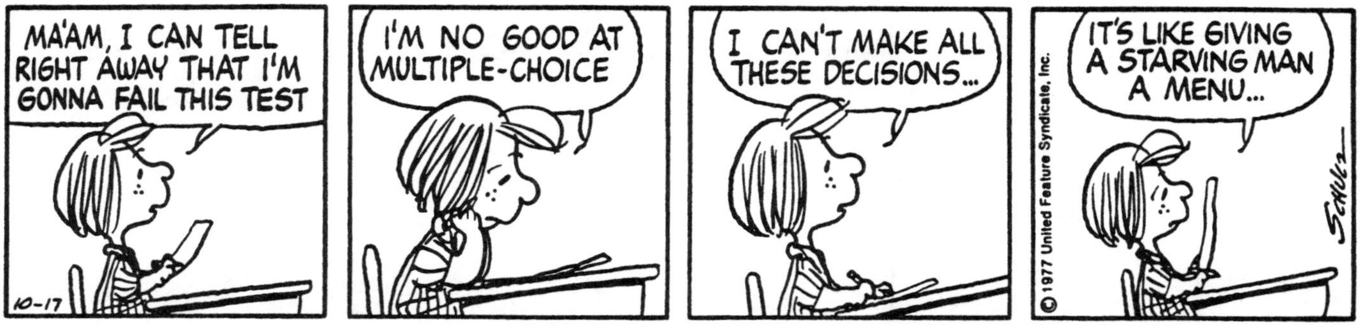
MA'AM, I CAN TELL RIGHT AWAY THAT I'M GONNA FAIL THIS TEST
10-17
I'M NO GOOD AT MULTIPLE-CHOICE
I CAN'T MAKE ALL THESE DECISIONS...
IT'S LIKE GIVING A STARVING MAN A MENU...
© 1977 United Feature Syndicate, Inc.
SCHULZ

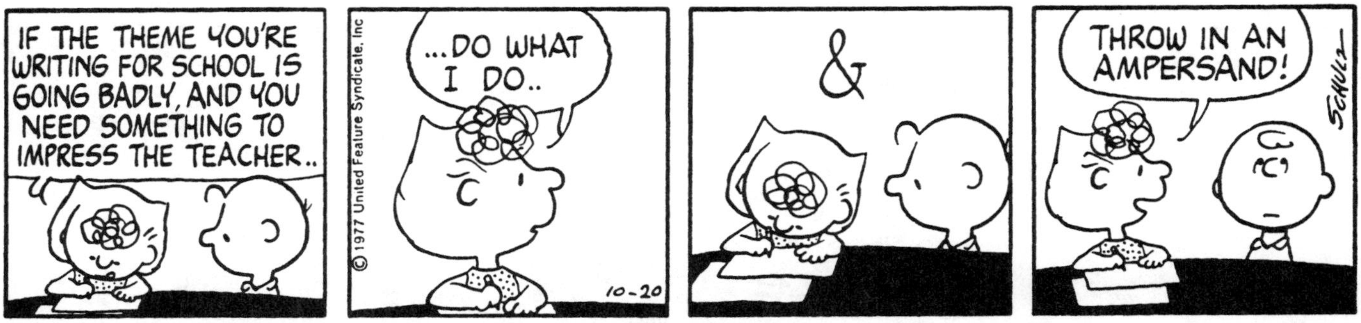
IF THE THEME YOU'RE WRITING FOR SCHOOL IS GOING BADLY, AND YOU NEED SOMETHING TO IMPRESS THE TEACHER..
© 1977 United Feature Syndicate, Inc
...DO WHAT I DO..
10-20
&
THROW IN AN AMPERSAND!
SCHULZ

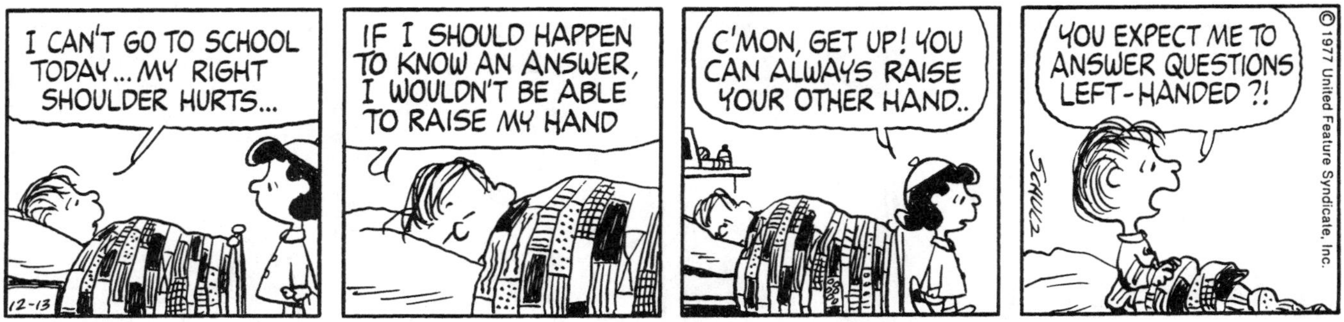
I CAN'T GO TO SCHOOL TODAY... MY RIGHT SHOULDER HURTS...
12-13
IF I SHOULD HAPPEN TO KNOW AN ANSWER, I WOULDN'T BE ABLE TO RAISE MY HAND
C'MON, GET UP! YOU CAN ALWAYS RAISE YOUR OTHER HAND..
SCHULZ
YOU EXPECT ME TO ANSWER QUESTIONS LEFT-HANDED?!
© 1977 United Feature Syndicate, Inc.

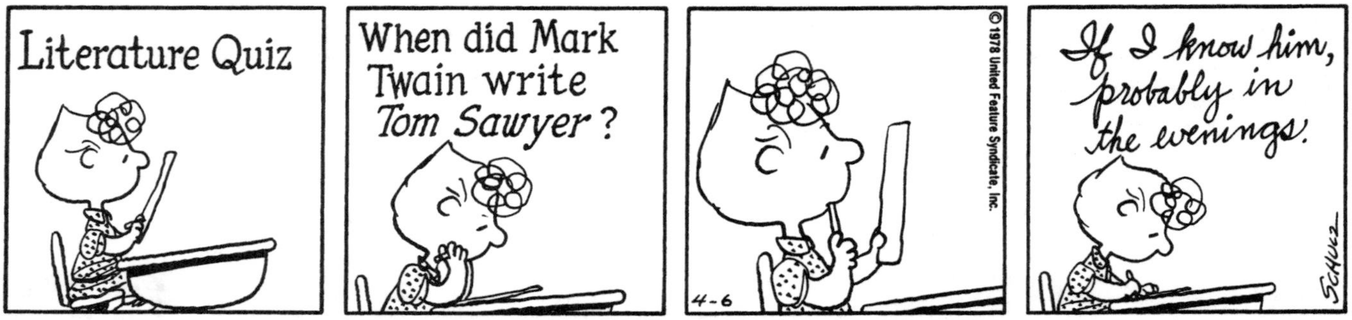
Literature Quiz
When did Mark Twain write *Tom Sawyer*?
© 1978 United Feature Syndicate, Inc.
4-6
If I know him, probably in the evenings.
SCHULZ

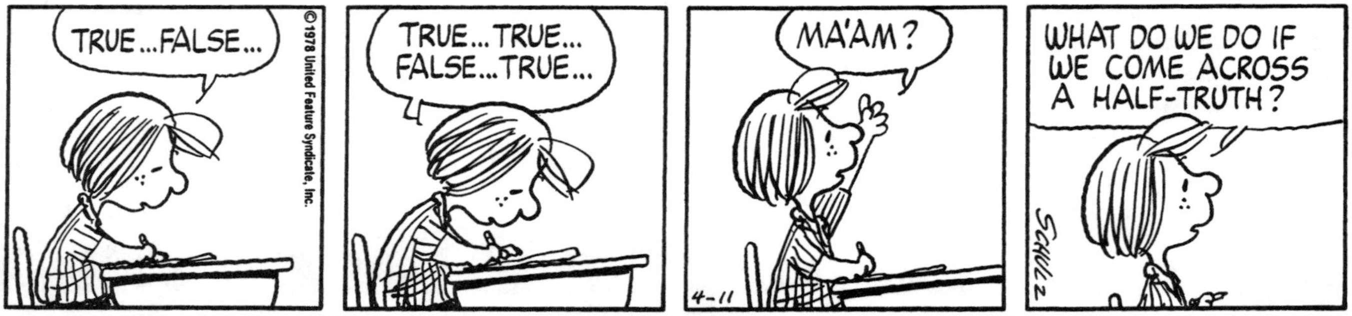
TRUE...FALSE...
© 1978 United Feature Syndicate, Inc.
TRUE...TRUE... FALSE...TRUE...
MA'AM?
4-11
WHAT DO WE DO IF WE COME ACROSS A HALF-TRUTH?
SCHULZ

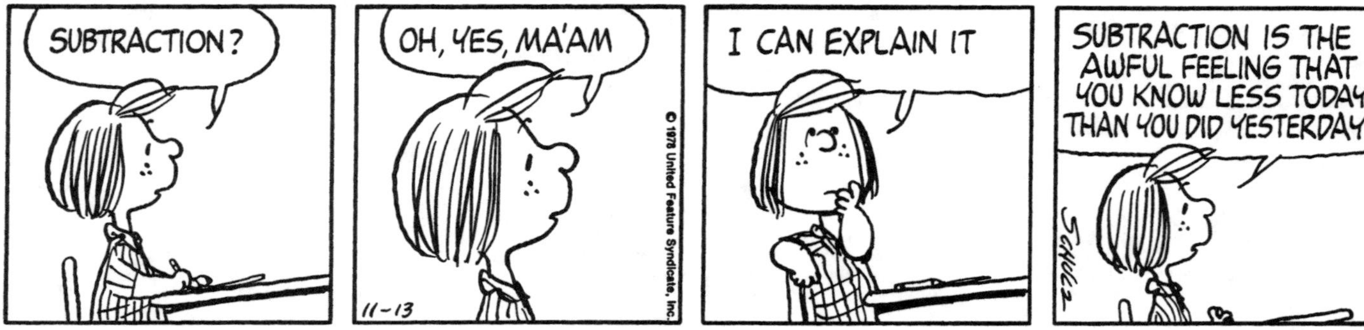
SUBTRACTION?
OH, YES, MA'AM
11-13
© 1978 United Feature Syndicate, Inc.
I CAN EXPLAIN IT
SUBTRACTION IS THE AWFUL FEELING THAT YOU KNOW LESS TODAY THAN YOU DID YESTERDAY
SCHULZ

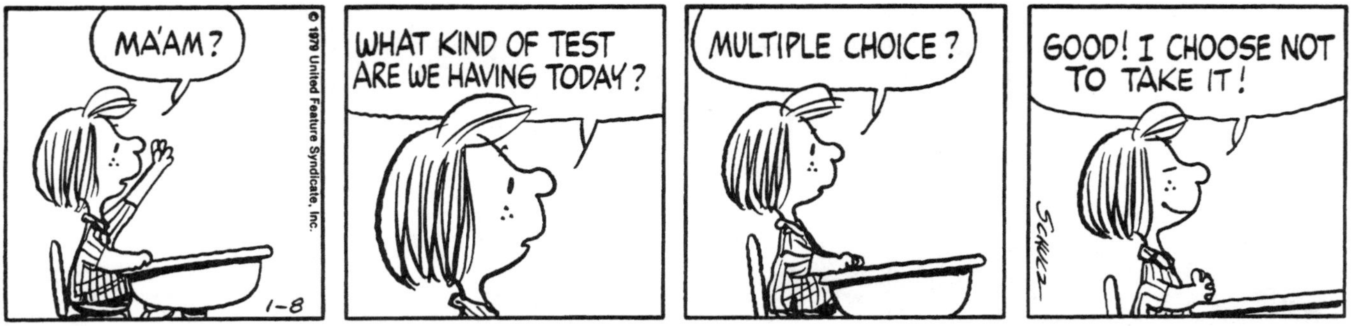
MA'AM?
© 1979 United Feature Syndicate, Inc.
1-8
WHAT KIND OF TEST ARE WE HAVING TODAY?
MULTIPLE CHOICE?
GOOD! I CHOOSE NOT TO TAKE IT!
SCHULZ

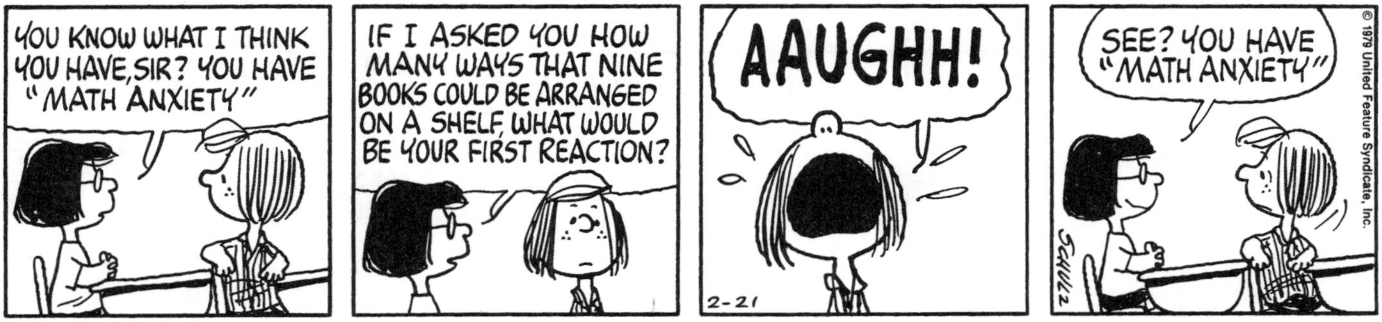
YOU KNOW WHAT I THINK YOU HAVE, SIR? YOU HAVE "MATH ANXIETY"
IF I ASKED YOU HOW MANY WAYS THAT NINE BOOKS COULD BE ARRANGED ON A SHELF, WHAT WOULD BE YOUR FIRST REACTION?
AAUGHH!
2-21
SEE? YOU HAVE "MATH ANXIETY"
© 1979 United Feature Syndicate, Inc.
SCHULZ

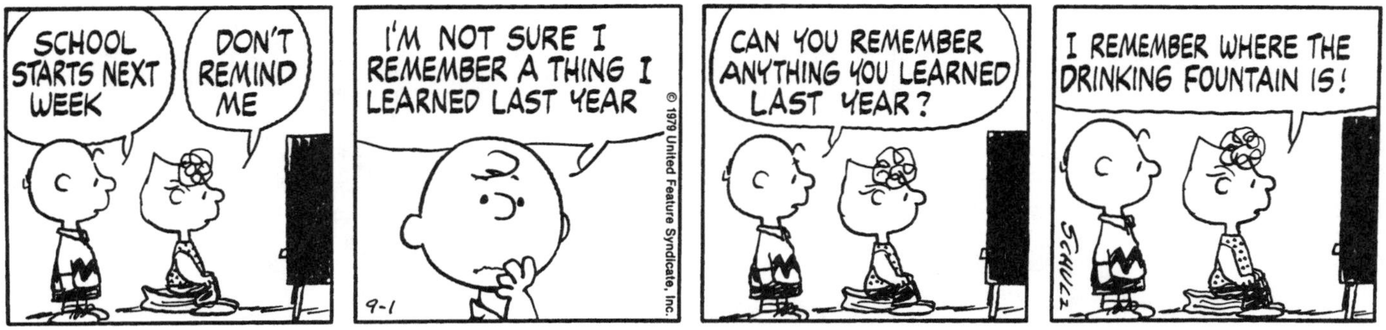
SCHOOL STARTS NEXT WEEK
DON'T REMIND ME
I'M NOT SURE I REMEMBER A THING I LEARNED LAST YEAR
9-1
© 1979 United Feature Syndicate, Inc.
CAN YOU REMEMBER ANYTHING YOU LEARNED LAST YEAR?
I REMEMBER WHERE THE DRINKING FOUNTAIN IS!
SCHULZ

I'VE GOT IT!

© 1979 United Feature Syndicate, Inc.

YES, MA'AM, I THINK I KNOW THE ANSWER

SIXTEEN.. FOUR.. THIRTY-SEVEN

9-12

ON SECOND THOUGHT, THAT MAY BE MY LOCKER COMBINATION!

© 1979 United Feature Syndicate, Inc.

WHO, ME?

9-21

YES, MA'AM, I THINK MY REPORT IS READY...

ANYWAY, I'LL GIVE IT MY BEST SHOT

JUST A LITTLE COLLOQUIALISM, THERE, MA'AM

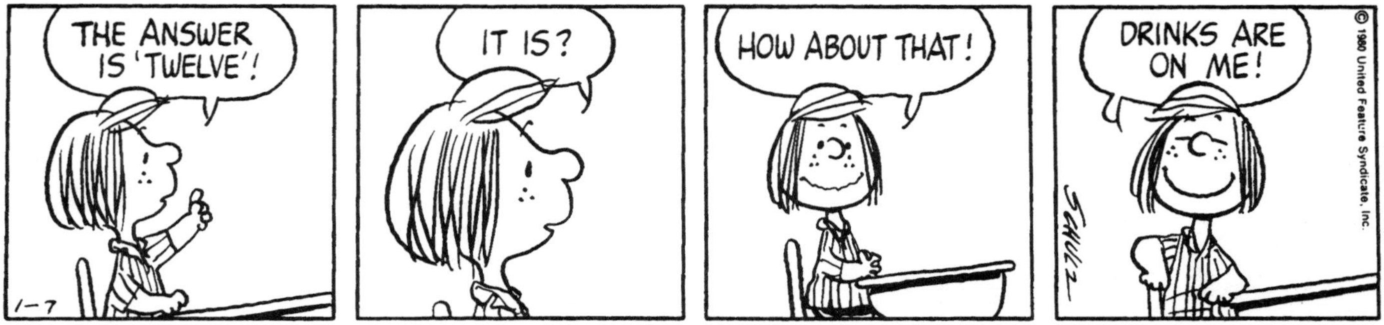
THE ANSWER IS 'TWELVE'!
IT IS?
HOW ABOUT THAT!
DRINKS ARE ON ME!
1-7
SCHULZ
© 1980 United Feature Syndicate, Inc.

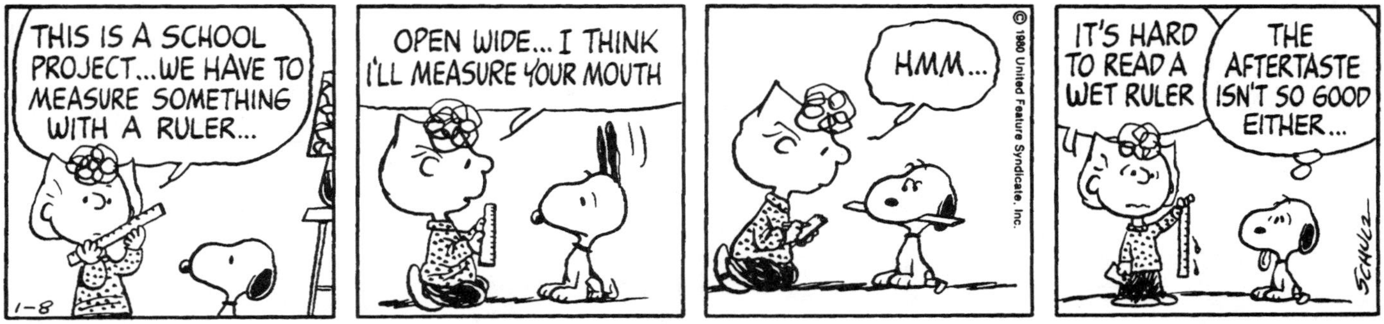
THIS IS A SCHOOL PROJECT...WE HAVE TO MEASURE SOMETHING WITH A RULER...
OPEN WIDE... I THINK I'LL MEASURE YOUR MOUTH
HMM...
IT'S HARD TO READ A WET RULER
THE AFTERTASTE ISN'T SO GOOD EITHER...
1-8
SCHULZ
© 1980 United Feature Syndicate, Inc.

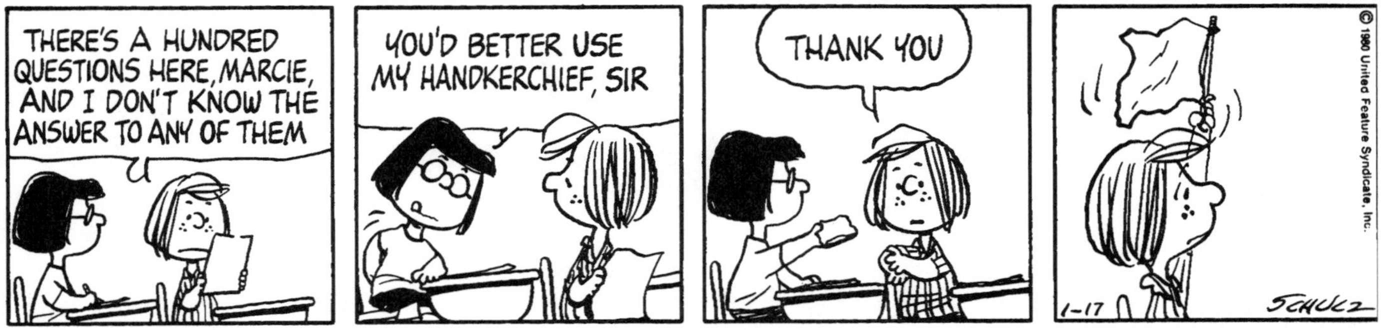
THERE'S A HUNDRED QUESTIONS HERE, MARCIE, AND I DON'T KNOW THE ANSWER TO ANY OF THEM
YOU'D BETTER USE MY HANDKERCHIEF, SIR
THANK YOU
1-17
SCHULZ
© 1980 United Feature Syndicate, Inc.

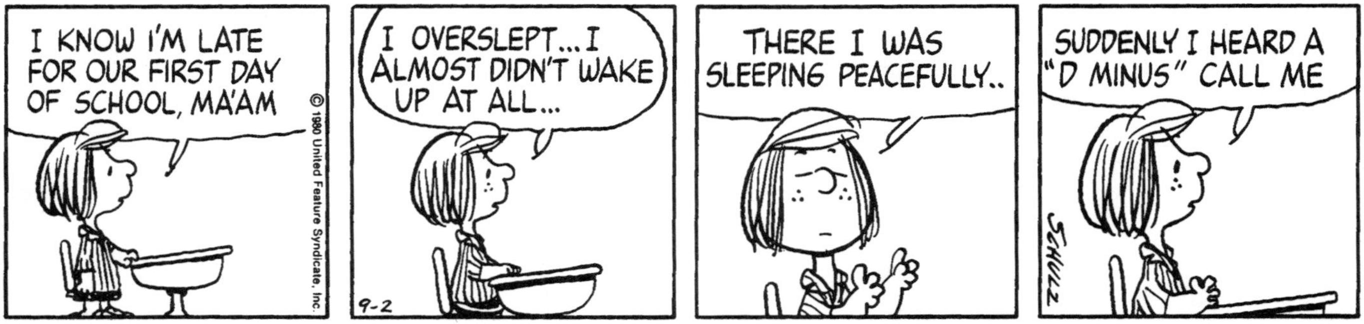
I KNOW I'M LATE FOR OUR FIRST DAY OF SCHOOL, MA'AM
I OVERSLEPT... I ALMOST DIDN'T WAKE UP AT ALL...
THERE I WAS SLEEPING PEACEFULLY..
SUDDENLY I HEARD A "D MINUS" CALL ME
9-2
SCHULZ
© 1980 United Feature Syndicate, Inc.

PSST! WAKE UP, SIR! YOU'RE MISSING THE HISTORY LESSON...
Z
9-8
WHEW!
HOW LONG DID I SLEEP, MARCIE?
FROM HENRY THE FOURTH TO HENRY THE SIXTH
© 1980 United Feature Syndicate, Inc.
SCHULZ

THAT'S A GOOD PAPER, SIR, BUT YOU DIDN'T USE ANY FOOTNOTES
WHY WOULD I NEED FOOTNOTES, MARCIE?
© 1980 United Feature Syndicate, Inc.
YOU USE A FOOTNOTE WHEN YOU GIVE THE SOURCE OF FACTS THAT ARE NOT COMMON KNOWLEDGE
10-14
THEN I'M OKAY.. I DON'T KNOW ANYTHING THAT'S NOT COMMON KNOWLEDGE
SCHULZ

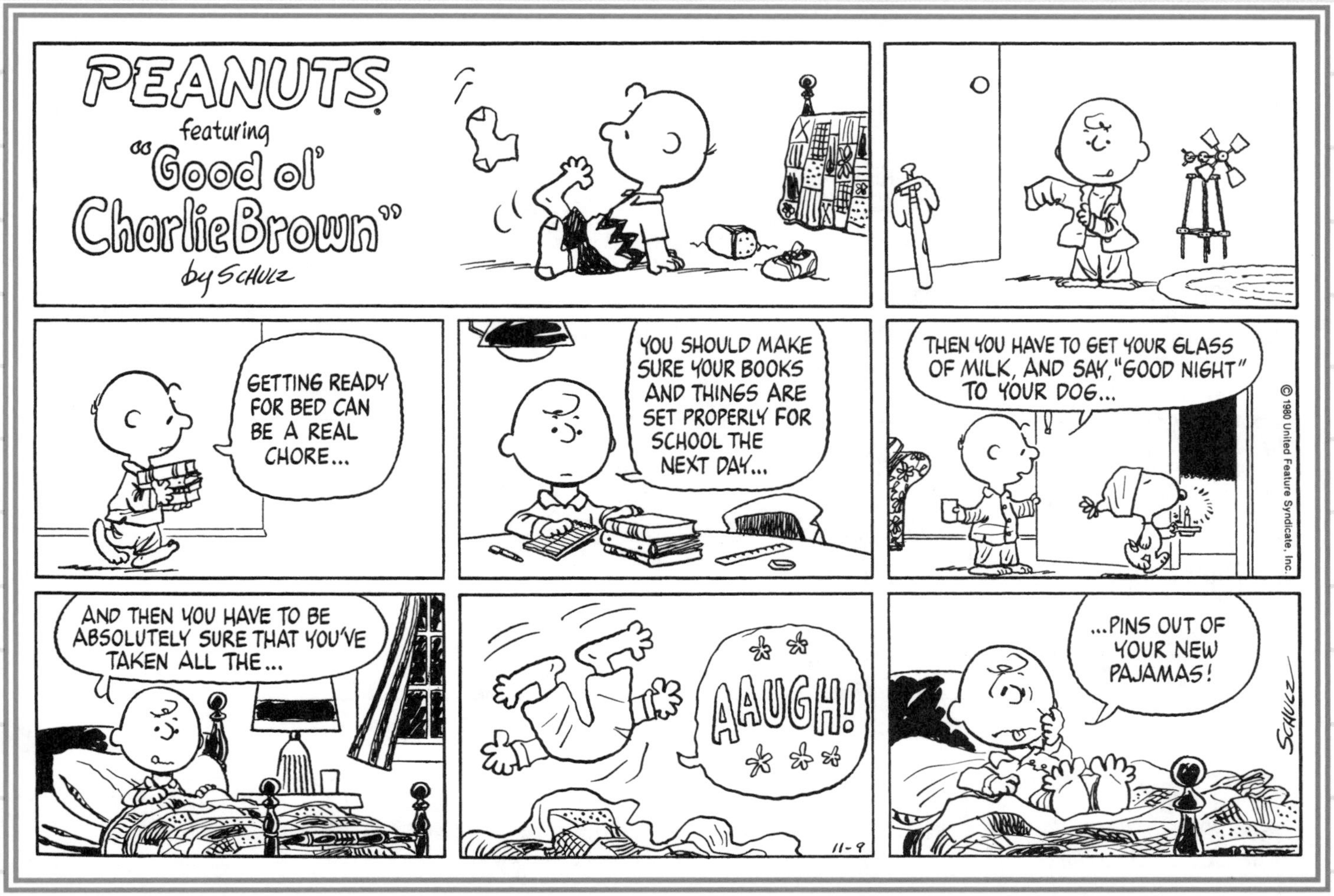
PEANUTS
featuring
"Good ol' Charlie Brown"
by SCHULZ
GETTING READY FOR BED CAN BE A REAL CHORE...
YOU SHOULD MAKE SURE YOUR BOOKS AND THINGS ARE SET PROPERLY FOR SCHOOL THE NEXT DAY...
THEN YOU HAVE TO GET YOUR GLASS OF MILK, AND SAY, "GOOD NIGHT" TO YOUR DOG...
© 1980 United Feature Syndicate, Inc.
AND THEN YOU HAVE TO BE ABSOLUTELY SURE THAT YOU'VE TAKEN ALL THE...
AAUGH!
11-9
...PINS OUT OF YOUR NEW PAJAMAS!
SCHULZ

IN CASE OF ILLNESS OR ACCIDENT, NOTIFY:
NAME ____
STREET ____ APT. ____
WHAT'S AN "APT," MARCIE? DON'T TELL ME! I'LL BET IT MEANS, "ARE YOU THE KIND WHO'S APT TO GET SICK?"
I'LL PUT DOWN A BIG "NO!"
© 1981 United Feature Syndicate, Inc.
GOOD THINKING, SIR
IT WASN'T HARD TO FIGURE OUT, MARCIE
SCHULZ
1-12

IT WAS A GREAT DAY IN THE YEAR 1605, MA'AM...
2-23
© 1981 United Feature Syndicate, Inc.
IT ALL HAPPENED IN ANTWERP
A PRINTER NAMED ABRAHAM VERKOEVEN BEGAN PUBLICATION OF THE FIRST NEWSPAPER...
SCHULZ
IMMEDIATELY PROMPTING TWELVE NASTY LETTERS TO THE EDITOR!

WHAT ARE YOU DOING UP SO EARLY?
I HAD TO FINISH THIS REPORT FOR SCHOOL..
IF I DON'T GET IT IN TODAY, I'M DOOMED!
HERE'S THE WORLD WAR I FLYING ACE DOWN BEHIND ENEMY LINES..HIS MISSION IS TO GET THE SECRET PAPERS...SUDDENLY, HE SEES HER...
THE RED BARON'S SECRETARY!
© 1981 United Feature Syndicate, Inc.
SCHULZ
3-12

GOOD FORTUNE SMILES ON THE WORLD WAR I FLYING ACE...
THE RED BARON'S SECRETARY HAS THE SECRET PAPERS...
© 1981 United Feature Syndicate, Inc.
HEY! WHAT ARE YOU DOING? THAT'S MY TERM PAPER!!!
NOT FOOLED BY THE GIRL'S SIMPLE CRIES, THE FLYING ACE DARTS SWIFTLY AWAY!
SCHULZ

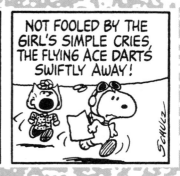

HERE'S THE WORLD WAR I FLYING ACE FLEEING FROM THE ENEMY WITH THE SECRET PAPERS...
YOU STUPID BEAGLE!! COME BACK HERE WITH MY TERM PAPER!!!
KNOWING HE IS ABOUT TO BE CAUGHT, HE BECOMES DESPERATE...
HE SWALLOWS THE PAPERS!
AAUGH!
© 1981 United Feature Syndicate, Inc.
SCHULZ

YOU STUPID BEAGLE!! YOU SWALLOWED MY TERM PAPER!
© 1981 United Feature Syndicate, Inc.
SORRY I'M LATE, MA'AM.. I HAD A LITTLE PROBLEM WITH MY TERM PAPER...
ANYWAY, HERE IT IS!
SCHULZ

3-17
YES, MA'AM? YOU WANT ME TO READ MY TERM PAPER TO THE CLASS?
OH, NO!
WELL, I MAY HAVE A LITTLE DIFFICULTY READING IT...
I SAID, " I MAY HAVE A LITTLE DIFFICULTY READING IT!!
© 1981 United Feature Syndicate, Inc.
SCHULZ
HOWEVER, I'LL SEE WHAT I CAN REMEMBER..
JUST HIT THE HIGH POINTS

IT'S A PHILOSOPHY, SIR..
IT SAYS THAT IF YOU DENY SOMETHING EXISTS, THEN IT DOESN'T EXIST
4/14
SORRY, MA'AM
SCHULZ
YOUR "D MINUSES" DON'T EXIST!
© 1981 United Feature Syndicate, Inc.

I CAN'T STAND IT... SCHOOL STARTS AGAIN IN TWO WEEKS...
MY FURLOUGH IS ALMOST OVER
8-25
© 1981 United Feature Syndicate, Inc.
YOU MEAN YOUR SUMMER VACATION
HOW LONG DO YOU HAVE TO BE IN BEFORE YOU GET SHORE LEAVE?
SCHULZ

HELLO, SCHOOL, HAVE YOU HAD A NICE SUMMER?
WE'LL ALL BE RETURNING IN ABOUT TWO WEEKS
8-26
SOMETIMES I WONDER WHY YOU WANT TO GO THROUGH THIS EVERY YEAR
IT'S THE ONLY THING I KNOW
SCHULZ
© 1981 United Feature Syndicate, Inc.

WHAT IF I GET TO SCHOOL NEXT WEEK, AND CAN'T REMEMBER MY LOCKER COMBINATION?
WHAT IF I FORGET MY LUNCH?
8-31
© 1981 United Feature Syndicate, Inc.
WHAT IF I CAN'T REMEMBER WHO MARRIED LOUIS THE MILLIONTH?
LOUIS THE MILLIONTH?
SCHULZ

YES, SIR..I NEED SOME SCHOOL SUPPLIES...
I NEED A NEW PEN, A BINDER, A PENCIL, A METRIC RULER, SOME PAPER AND...
9-4
© 1981 United Feature Syndicate, Inc.
AND WHAT ELSE? OH, YES...
A LOT OF LUCK!
SCHULZ

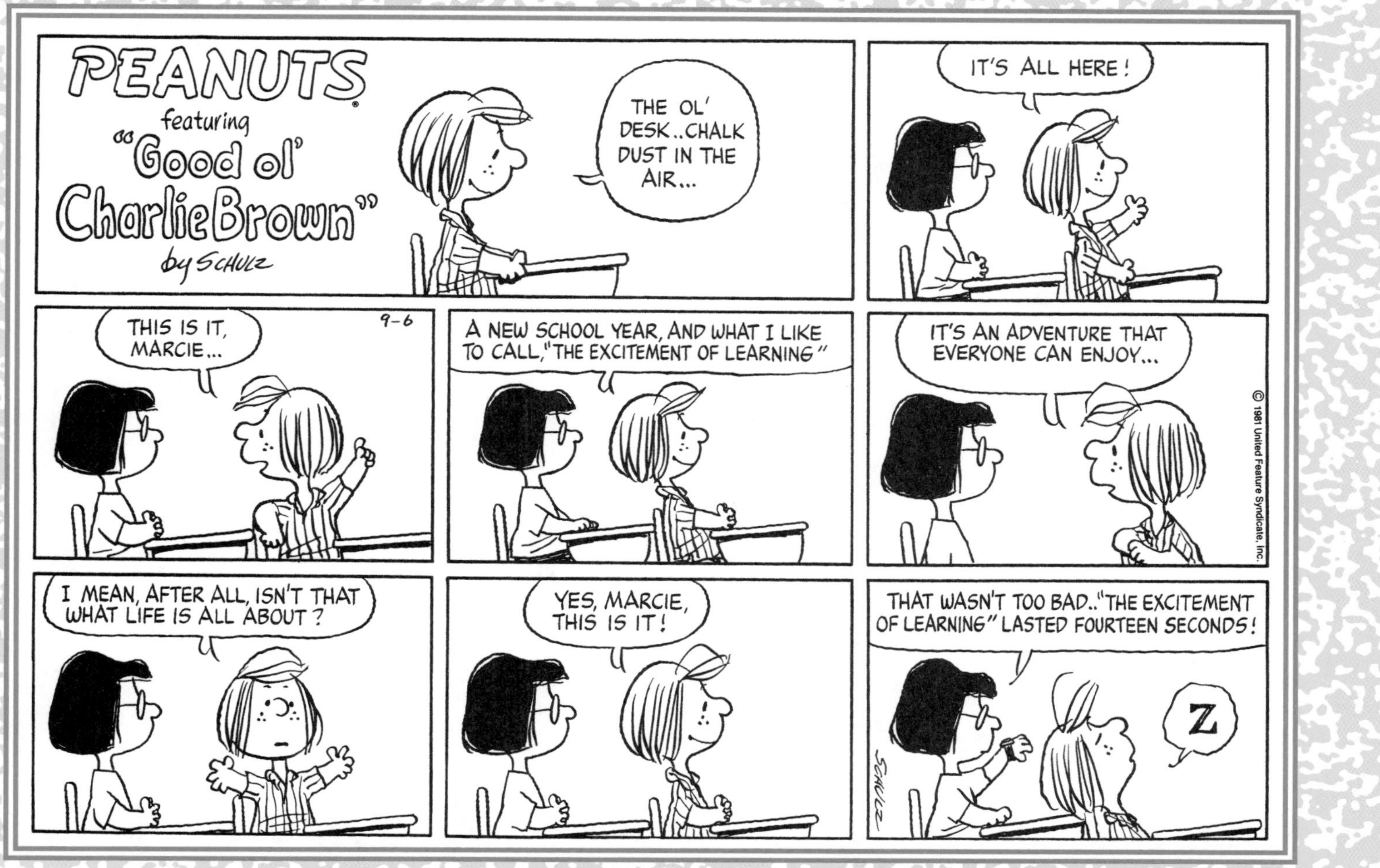
PEANUTS
featuring
"Good ol' Charlie Brown"
by SCHULZ
THE OL' DESK..CHALK DUST IN THE AIR...
IT'S ALL HERE!
9-6
THIS IS IT, MARCIE...
A NEW SCHOOL YEAR, AND WHAT I LIKE TO CALL, "THE EXCITEMENT OF LEARNING"
IT'S AN ADVENTURE THAT EVERYONE CAN ENJOY...
© 1981 United Feature Syndicate, Inc.
I MEAN, AFTER ALL, ISN'T THAT WHAT LIFE IS ALL ABOUT?
YES, MARCIE, THIS IS IT!
THAT WASN'T TOO BAD.."THE EXCITEMENT OF LEARNING" LASTED FOURTEEN SECONDS!
Z
SCHULZ

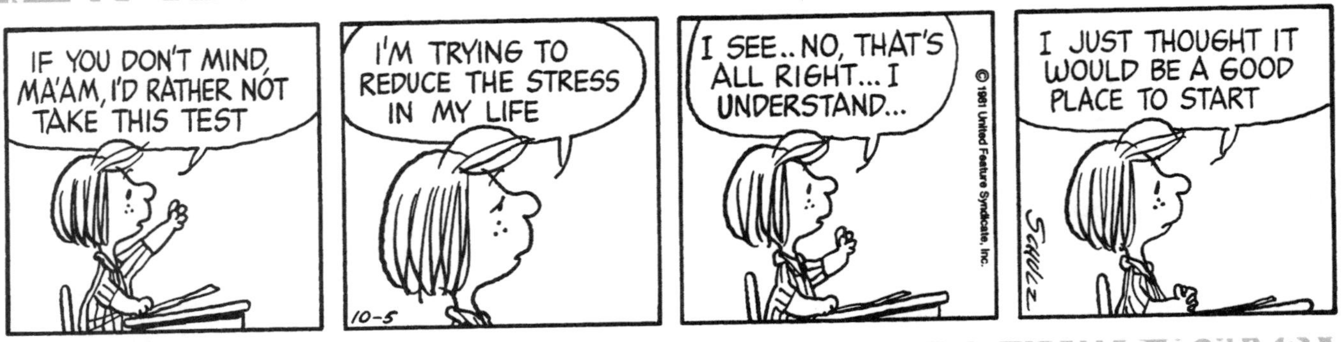
IF YOU DON'T MIND, MA'AM, I'D RATHER NOT TAKE THIS TEST
I'M TRYING TO REDUCE THE STRESS IN MY LIFE
10-5
I SEE.. NO, THAT'S ALL RIGHT... I UNDERSTAND...
© 1981 United Feature Syndicate, Inc.
I JUST THOUGHT IT WOULD BE A GOOD PLACE TO START
SCHULZ

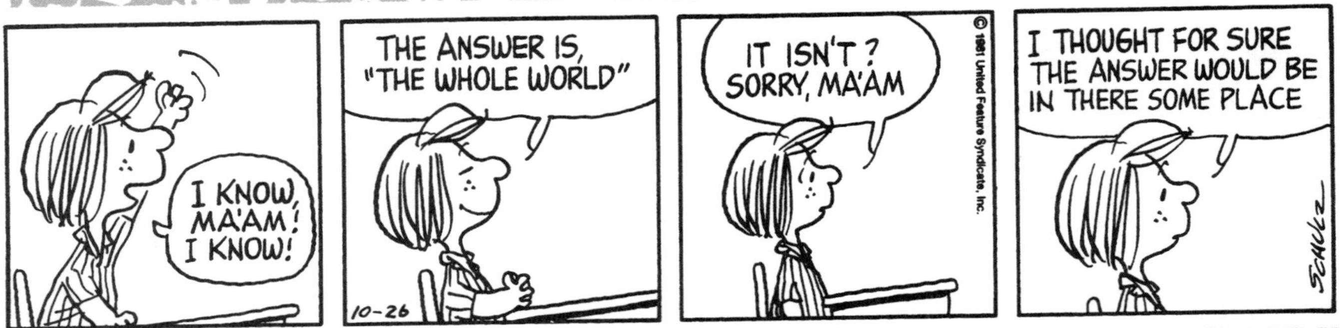
I KNOW, MA'AM! I KNOW!
THE ANSWER IS, "THE WHOLE WORLD"
10-26
IT ISN'T? SORRY, MA'AM
© 1981 United Feature Syndicate, Inc.
I THOUGHT FOR SURE THE ANSWER WOULD BE IN THERE SOME PLACE
SCHULZ

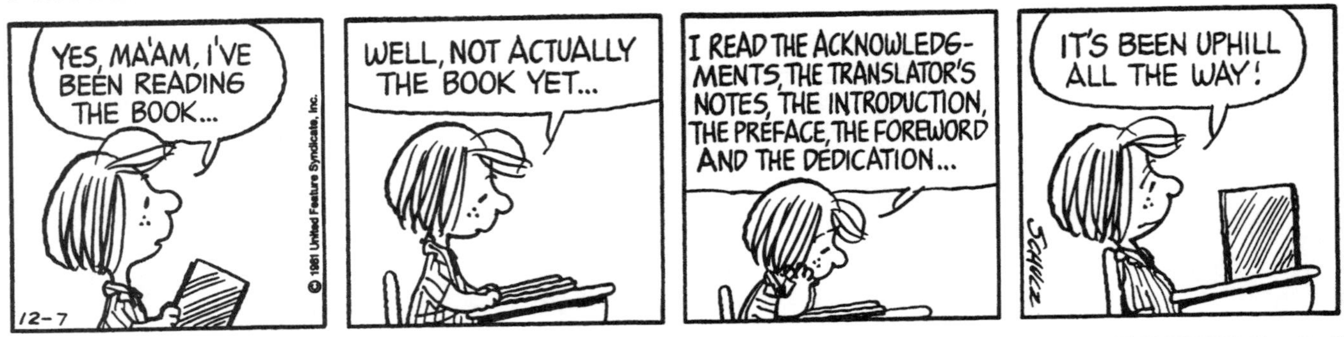
YES, MA'AM, I'VE BEEN READING THE BOOK...
12-7
© 1981 United Feature Syndicate, Inc.
WELL, NOT ACTUALLY THE BOOK YET...
I READ THE ACKNOWLEDGMENTS, THE TRANSLATOR'S NOTES, THE INTRODUCTION, THE PREFACE, THE FOREWORD AND THE DEDICATION...
IT'S BEEN UPHILL ALL THE WAY!
SCHULZ

I'LL SAY, "THREE"
3-25
I WAS RIGHT?
© 1982 United Feature Syndicate, Inc.
I KNEW IT!
SCHULZ

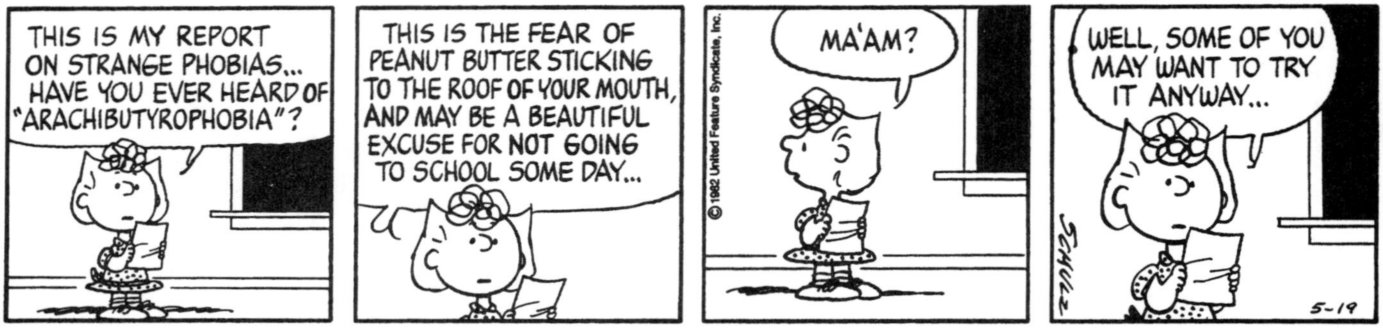
THIS IS MY REPORT ON STRANGE PHOBIAS... HAVE YOU EVER HEARD OF "ARACHIBUTYROPHOBIA"?
THIS IS THE FEAR OF PEANUT BUTTER STICKING TO THE ROOF OF YOUR MOUTH, AND MAY BE A BEAUTIFUL EXCUSE FOR NOT GOING TO SCHOOL SOME DAY...
© 1982 United Feature Syndicate, Inc.
MA'AM?
WELL, SOME OF YOU MAY WANT TO TRY IT ANYWAY...
SCHULZ
5-19

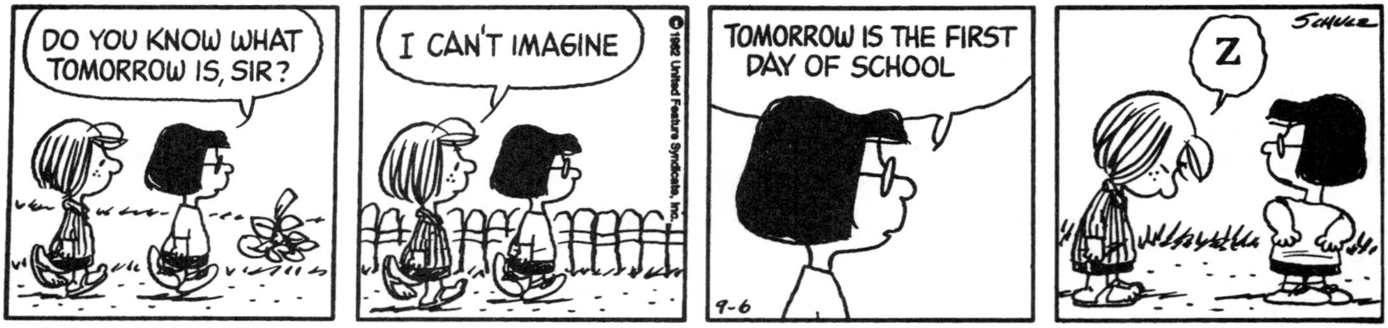
DO YOU KNOW WHAT TOMORROW IS, SIR?
I CAN'T IMAGINE
© 1982 United Feature Syndicate, Inc.
TOMORROW IS THE FIRST DAY OF SCHOOL
9-6
SCHULZ
Z

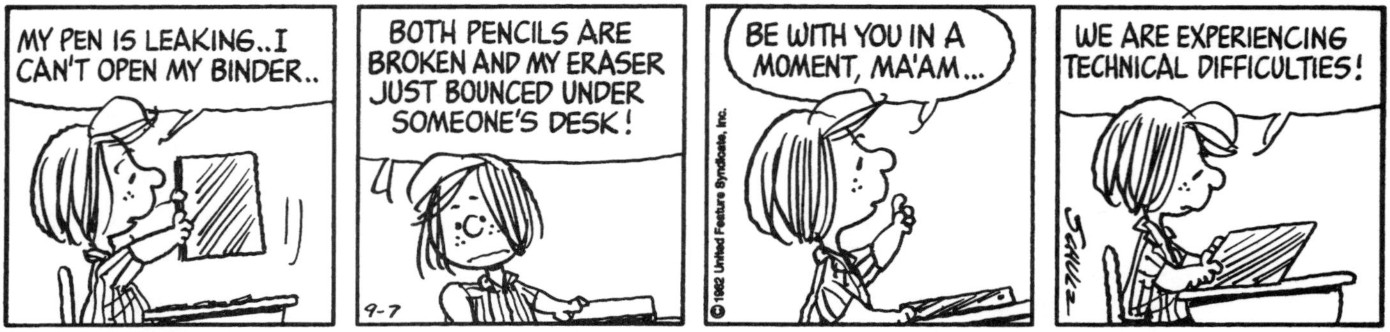
MY PEN IS LEAKING..I CAN'T OPEN MY BINDER..
BOTH PENCILS ARE BROKEN AND MY ERASER JUST BOUNCED UNDER SOMEONE'S DESK!
9-7
BE WITH YOU IN A MOMENT, MA'AM...
© 1982 United Feature Syndicate, Inc.
WE ARE EXPERIENCING TECHNICAL DIFFICULTIES!
SCHULZ

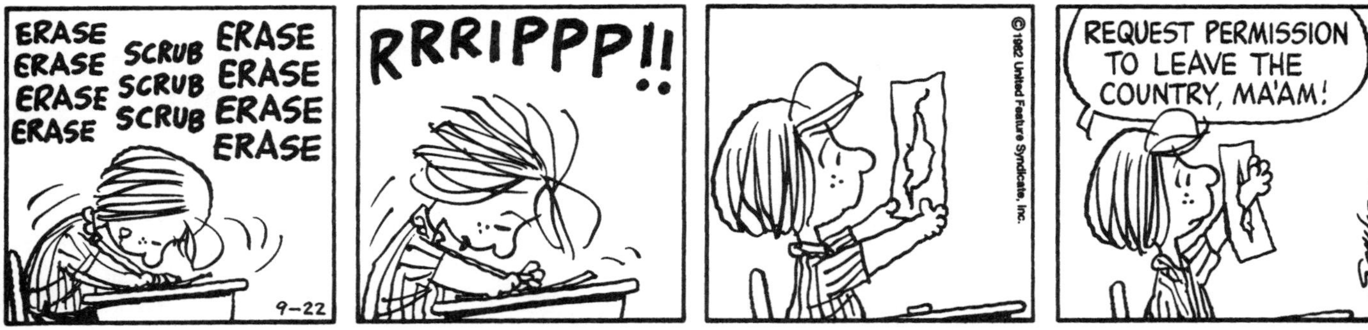
ERASE ERASE ERASE ERASE SCRUB SCRUB SCRUB ERASE ERASE ERASE ERASE
9-22
RRRIPPP!!
© 1982 United Feature Syndicate, Inc.
REQUEST PERMISSION TO LEAVE THE COUNTRY, MA'AM!

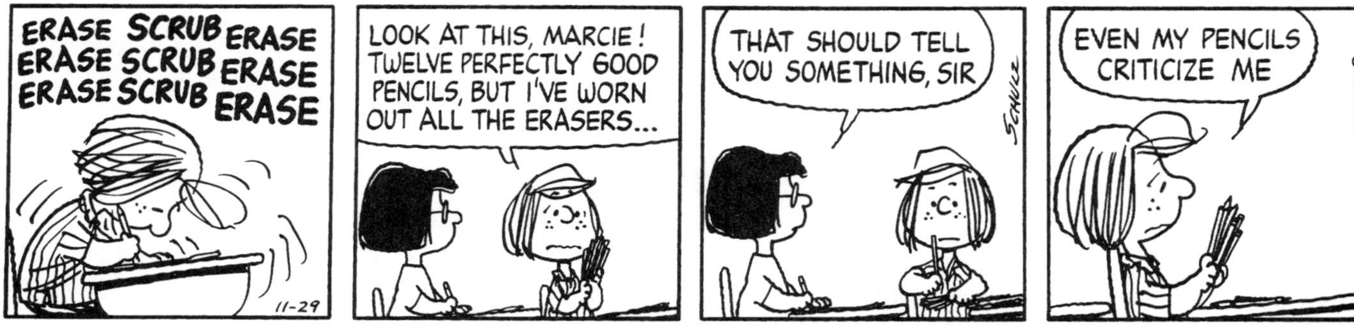
ERASE SCRUB ERASE ERASE SCRUB ERASE ERASE SCRUB ERASE
11-29
LOOK AT THIS, MARCIE! TWELVE PERFECTLY GOOD PENCILS, BUT I'VE WORN OUT ALL THE ERASERS...
THAT SHOULD TELL YOU SOMETHING, SIR
EVEN MY PENCILS CRITICIZE ME
© 1982 United Feature Syndicate, Inc.

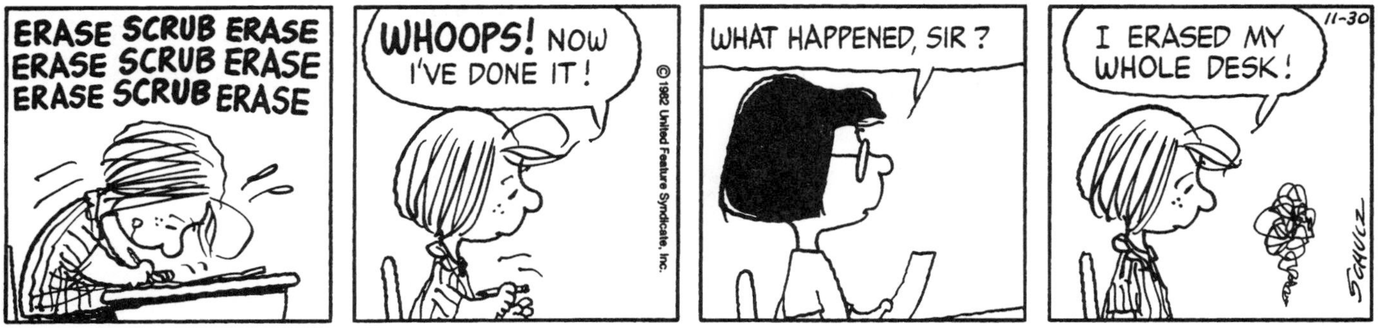
ERASE SCRUB ERASE ERASE SCRUB ERASE ERASE SCRUB ERASE
WHOOPS! NOW I'VE DONE IT!
© 1982 United Feature Syndicate, Inc.
WHAT HAPPENED, SIR?
11-30
I ERASED MY WHOLE DESK!

ALL MY LIFE I HAVE SEARCHED FOR CALMNESS
© 1983 United Feature Syndicate, Inc.
IT WAS A DIFFICULT STRUGGLE, BUT IT WAS WORTH IT..NOW I HAVE A BEAUTIFUL INNER PEACE
8-30
THERE IS NOTHING ANYONE CAN SAY OR DO THAT CAN DISTURB MY CALMNESS...
SCHOOL STARTS NEXT WEEK
AAUGH!

PEANUTS
featuring
"Good ol' Charlie Brown"
by SCHULZ
my Report
DON'T ASK!
?
NOT SO FAST, MARCIE.. SLOW DOWN...
YES, MA'AM, I GOT MY FOOT CAUGHT IN MY BINDER...
I HAD TO HOP ALL THE WAY TO SCHOOL ON ONE FOOT... LIKE THIS...
© 1983 United Feature Syndicate, Inc.
YES, MA'AM, I KNOW.. I'VE HAD MY FINGERS, MY NOSE AND MY HAIR CAUGHT... AND NOW MY FOOT...
9-11
MY REPORT? WELL, IT'S IN THE BINDER... I'LL TRY TO GET IT OFF... THERE!! WHEW!
NOW I'LL JUST LEAVE THE RINGS OPEN AND TAKE MY REPORT TO YOU AND PLACE THE BINDER ON YOUR DESK... CAREFUL, MA'AM...
SNAP
SCHULZ
SORT OF SMARTS, DOESN'T IT, MA'AM?

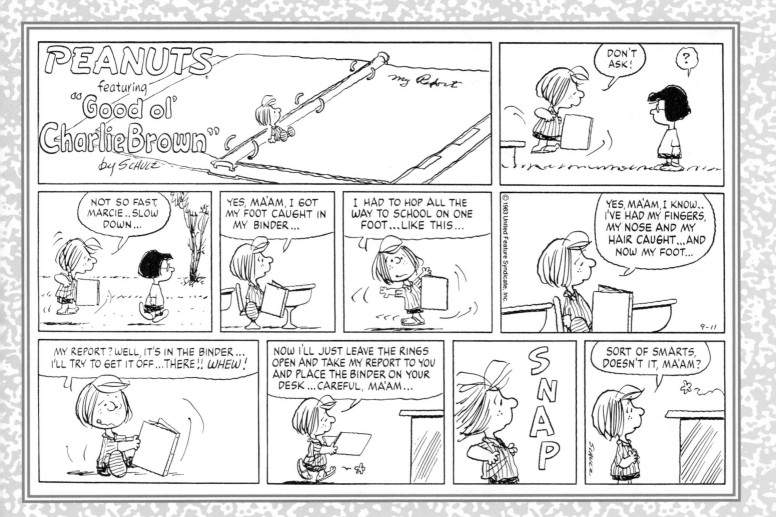

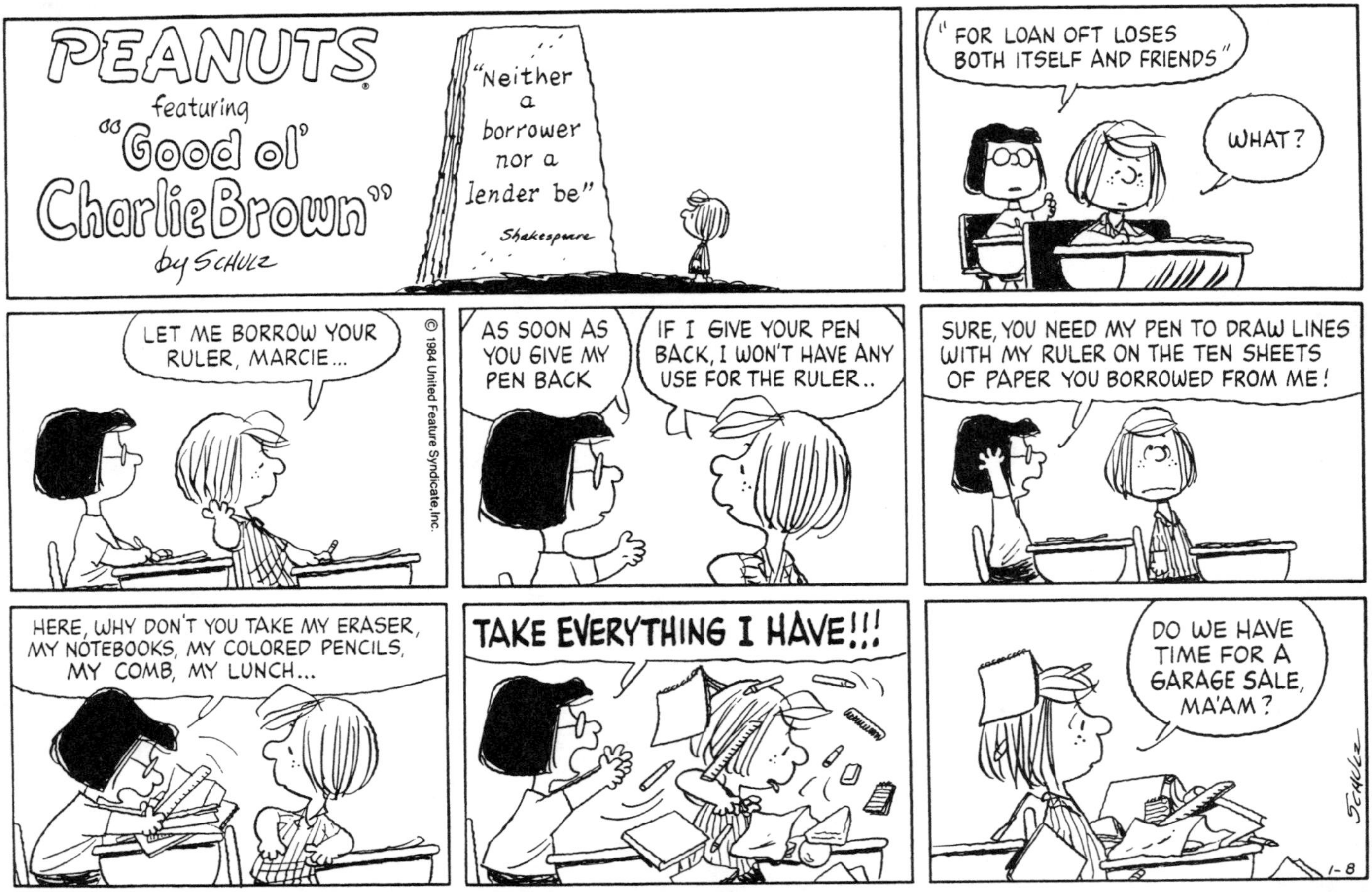
PEANUTS
featuring "Good ol' CharlieBrown"
by SCHULZ
"Neither a borrower nor a lender be"
Shakespeare
" FOR LOAN OFT LOSES BOTH ITSELF AND FRIENDS "
WHAT?
LET ME BORROW YOUR RULER, MARCIE...
© 1984 United Feature Syndicate, Inc.
AS SOON AS YOU GIVE MY PEN BACK
IF I GIVE YOUR PEN BACK, I WON'T HAVE ANY USE FOR THE RULER..
SURE, YOU NEED MY PEN TO DRAW LINES WITH MY RULER ON THE TEN SHEETS OF PAPER YOU BORROWED FROM ME!
HERE, WHY DON'T YOU TAKE MY ERASER, MY NOTEBOOKS, MY COLORED PENCILS, MY COMB, MY LUNCH...
TAKE EVERYTHING I HAVE!!!
DO WE HAVE TIME FOR A GARAGE SALE, MA'AM?
SCHULZ
1-8

WHY CAN'T I WEAR THIS SHIRT TO SCHOOL?
AND I WANNA WEAR MY BOOTS! WHY CAN'T I WEAR MY BOOTS?
1-9
© 1984 United Feature Syndicate, Inc.
I SUPPOSE YOU WANT ME TO WEAR HUMAN CLOTHES!
SCHULZ

AND THAT'S THE WAY I SEE IT! ABSOLUTELY, FOR SURE!
2-23
ACTUALLY, YOU HAVE YOUR FACTS MIXED UP, CHARLIE BROWN...
© 1984 United Feature Syndicate,Inc.
I DO? I GUESS MAYBE YOU'RE RIGHT
I HAVE VERY STRONG OPINIONS, BUT THEY DON'T LAST LONG!
SCHULZ

ONE "ROD" EQUALS NINE FEET...ONE "SPAN" EQUALS NINE INCHES...
ONE "PACE" EQUALS THREE FEET... ONE "HANDBREADTH" EQUALS THREE INCHES...
© 1984 United Feature Syndicate,Inc.
AND ONE "SCHOOL DAY" EQUALS A HUNDRED YEARS!
5-9
SORRY, MA'AM, I COULDN'T HELP SLIPPING THAT IN THERE...
SCHULZ

SCHOOL STARTS SOON, FRANKLIN, BUT WE WON'T BE IN THE SAME CLASS THIS TERM...
I'M GONNA MISS YOU, PATRICIA..
© 1984 United Feature Syndicate,Inc.
I REMEMBER ONCE I THOUGHT I HEARD A JET FLYING OVER OUR SCHOOL..I TURNED AROUND, AND IT WAS YOU SNORING...
8-29
DON'T COUNT ON ME SPEAKING TO YOU AT THE HIGH SCHOOL PROM, FRANKLIN!
SCHULZ

I THINK YOU CAN DO BETTER IN SCHOOL THIS YEAR, SIR..I THINK YOU CAN GET STRAIGHT A'S!
8-30
I BELIEVE IN YOU, SIR! I KNOW YOU CAN DO IT! I KNOW YOU CAN GET STRAIGHT A'S!
WELL, MAYBE I'LL TAKE THAT BACK..
I THINK YOU CAN
YOU'RE WEIRD, MARCIE
SCHULZ
© 1984 United Feature Syndicate,Inc.

SCHOOL STARTS TOMORROW, SIR...ARE YOU READY?
I'M READY, MARCIE.. I ALREADY KNOW ALL THE ANSWERS...
© 1984 United Feature Syndicate,Inc.
9-3
YOU DIDN'T KNOW MANY LAST YEAR
SO THIS YEAR TRUES WILL BE FALSE AND FALSES WILL BE TRUE!
YOU'RE WEIRD, SIR!
SCHULZ

PATRICIA? YES, MA'AM..
© 1984 United Feature Syndicate,Inc.
9-4
THAT'S ME
I'M THE ONE WHO FAILED LAST YEAR
SCHULZ
FASTEN YOUR SEAT BELT, MA'AM...HERE I COME AGAIN!

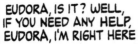

EUDORA, IS IT? WELL, IF YOU NEED ANY HELP, EUDORA, I'M RIGHT HERE
I TOOK ALL OF THESE CLASSES LAST YEAR SO I KNOW ALL THE ANSWERS
JUST DO WHAT I DO, EUDORA, AND YOU'LL GET ALONG GREAT!
Z
Z
© 1984 United Feature Syndicate, Inc.

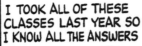

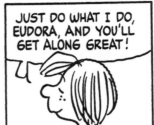

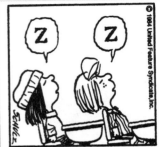

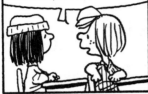

YOU'RE SITTING IN MY DESK, KID...HOW ABOUT MOVING?
© 1984 United Feature Syndicate, Inc.
OH, YOU'RE THE DUMB ONE WHO FAILED LAST YEAR, AREN'T YOU?
WATCH FOR YOU AND ME ON TV, KID...
THE PROGRAM IS CALLED "BOWL A PUPIL"!

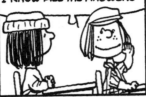

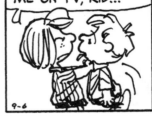

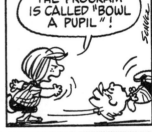

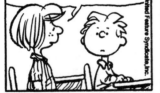

YES, SIR, MR.PRINCIPAL... MY NAME IS PATRICIA..
SCHOOL HAS JUST STARTED, AND I'M IN TROUBLE ALREADY, HUH?
WELL, THIS KID SORT OF INSULTED ME SO I KIND OF BOWLED HIM DOWN THE AISLE..I SHOULDN'T HAVE DONE THAT, HUH?
DO YOU HAVE A PENALTY BOX?
© 1984 United Feature Syndicate, Inc.

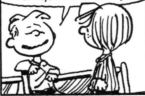

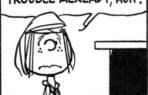

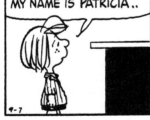

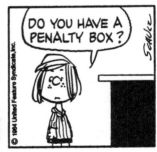

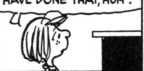

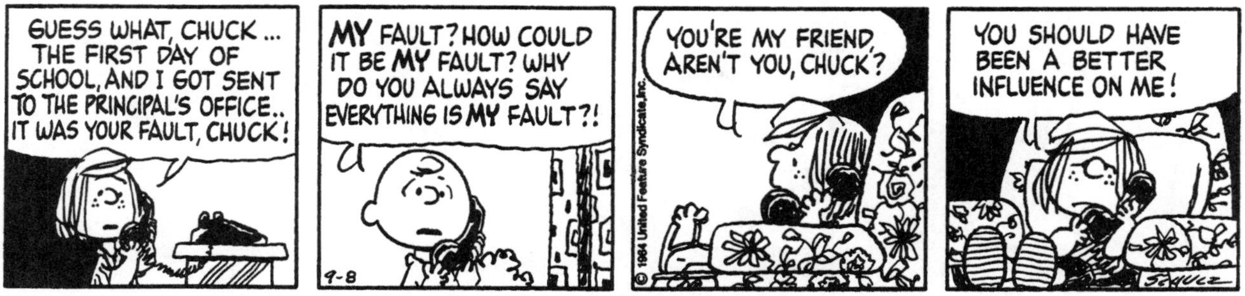
GUESS WHAT, CHUCK ... THE FIRST DAY OF SCHOOL, AND I GOT SENT TO THE PRINCIPAL'S OFFICE.. IT WAS YOUR FAULT, CHUCK!
MY FAULT? HOW COULD IT BE MY FAULT? WHY DO YOU ALWAYS SAY EVERYTHING IS MY FAULT?!
9-8
YOU'RE MY FRIEND, AREN'T YOU, CHUCK?
© 1984 United Feature Syndicate, Inc.
YOU SHOULD HAVE BEEN A BETTER INFLUENCE ON ME!
SCHULZ

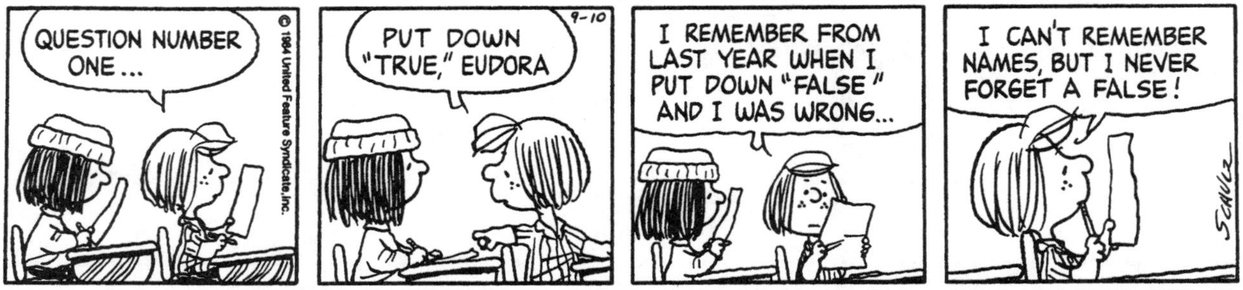
QUESTION NUMBER ONE ...
© 1984 United Feature Syndicate, Inc.
PUT DOWN "TRUE," EUDORA
9-10
I REMEMBER FROM LAST YEAR WHEN I PUT DOWN "FALSE" AND I WAS WRONG...
I CAN'T REMEMBER NAMES, BUT I NEVER FORGET A FALSE!
SCHULZ

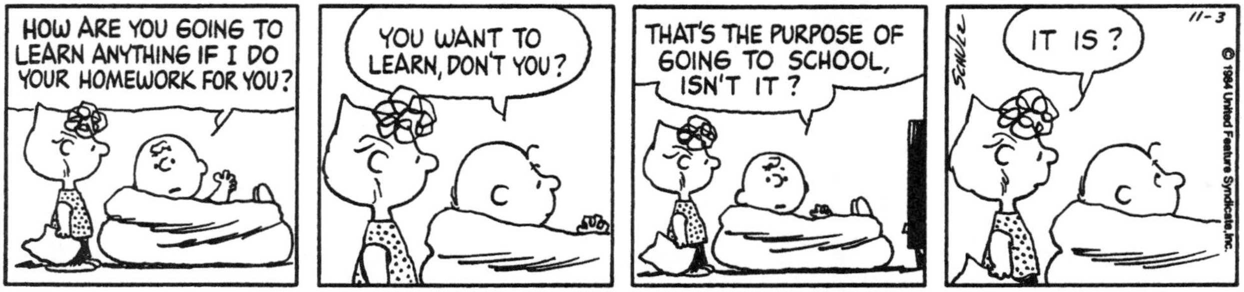
HOW ARE YOU GOING TO LEARN ANYTHING IF I DO YOUR HOMEWORK FOR YOU?
YOU WANT TO LEARN, DON'T YOU?
THAT'S THE PURPOSE OF GOING TO SCHOOL, ISN'T IT?
SCHULZ
IT IS?
11-3
© 1984 United Feature Syndicate, Inc.

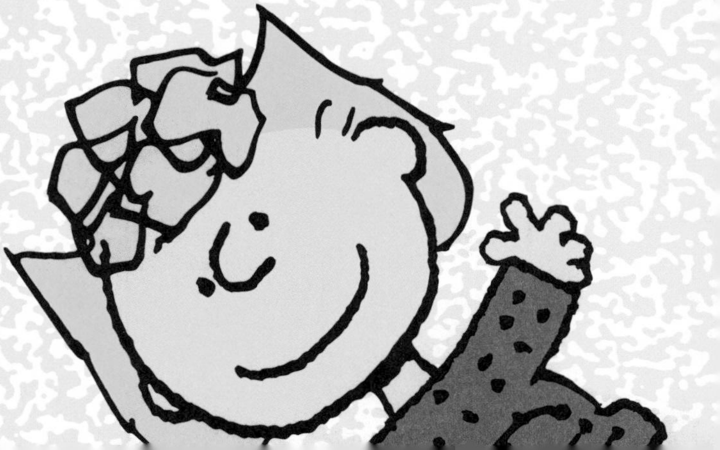

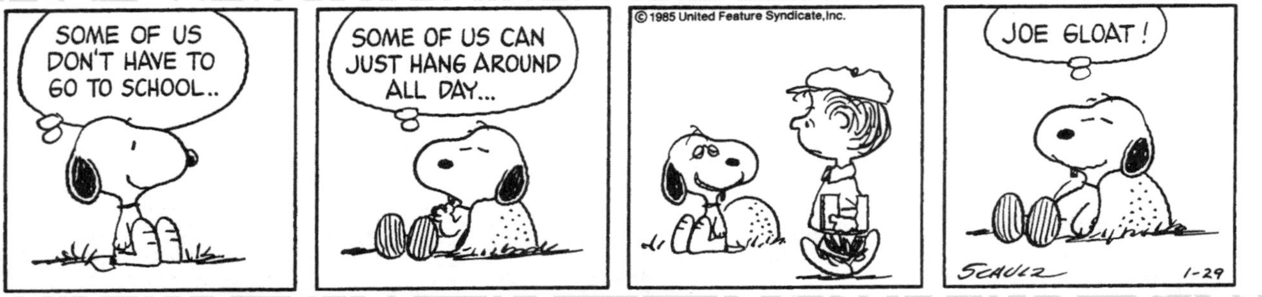
SOME OF US DON'T HAVE TO GO TO SCHOOL..
SOME OF US CAN JUST HANG AROUND ALL DAY...
© 1985 United Feature Syndicate, Inc.
JOE GLOAT!
SCHULZ
1-29

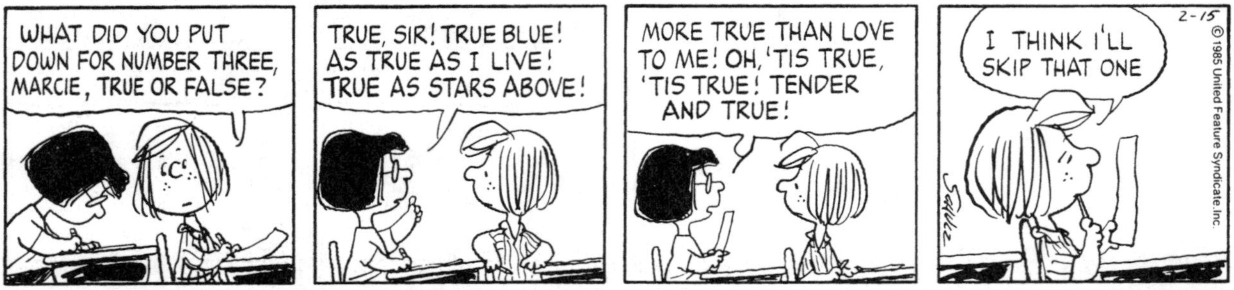
WHAT DID YOU PUT DOWN FOR NUMBER THREE, MARCIE, TRUE OR FALSE?
TRUE, SIR! TRUE BLUE! AS TRUE AS I LIVE! TRUE AS STARS ABOVE!
MORE TRUE THAN LOVE TO ME! OH, 'TIS TRUE, 'TIS TRUE! TENDER AND TRUE!
2-15
I THINK I'LL SKIP THAT ONE
SCHULZ
© 1985 United Feature Syndicate, Inc.

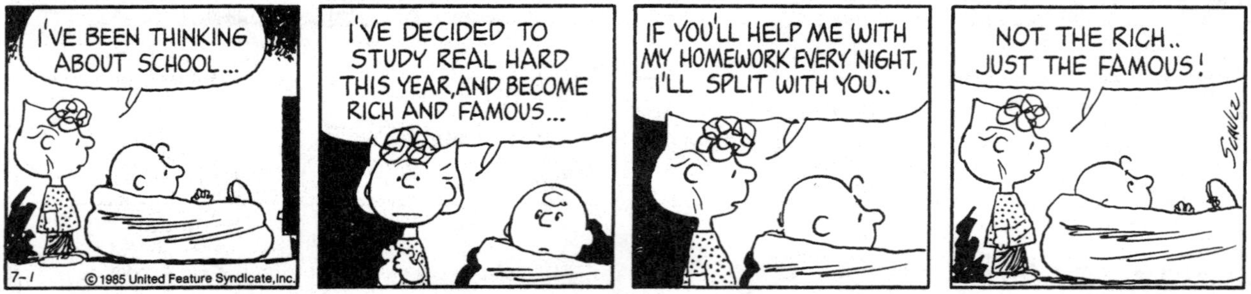
I'VE BEEN THINKING ABOUT SCHOOL...
7-1
© 1985 United Feature Syndicate, Inc.
I'VE DECIDED TO STUDY REAL HARD THIS YEAR, AND BECOME RICH AND FAMOUS...
IF YOU'LL HELP ME WITH MY HOMEWORK EVERY NIGHT, I'LL SPLIT WITH YOU..
NOT THE RICH.. JUST THE FAMOUS!
SCHULZ

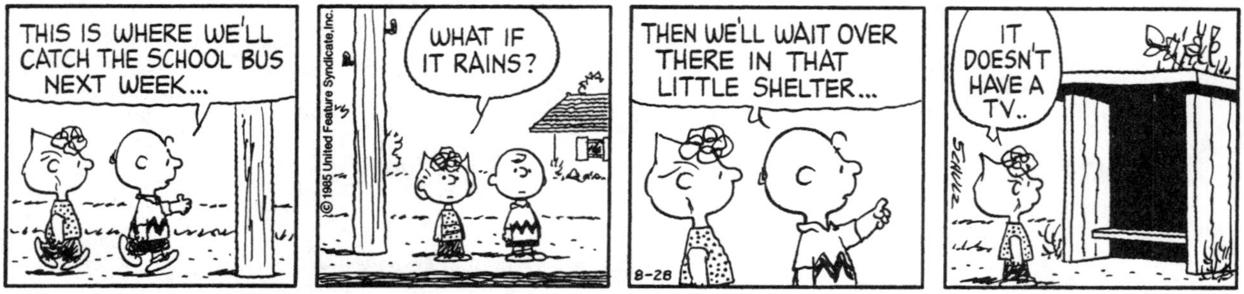
THIS IS WHERE WE'LL CATCH THE SCHOOL BUS NEXT WEEK...
© 1985 United Feature Syndicate, Inc.
WHAT IF IT RAINS?
THEN WE'LL WAIT OVER THERE IN THAT LITTLE SHELTER...
8-28
IT DOESN'T HAVE A TV..
SCHULZ

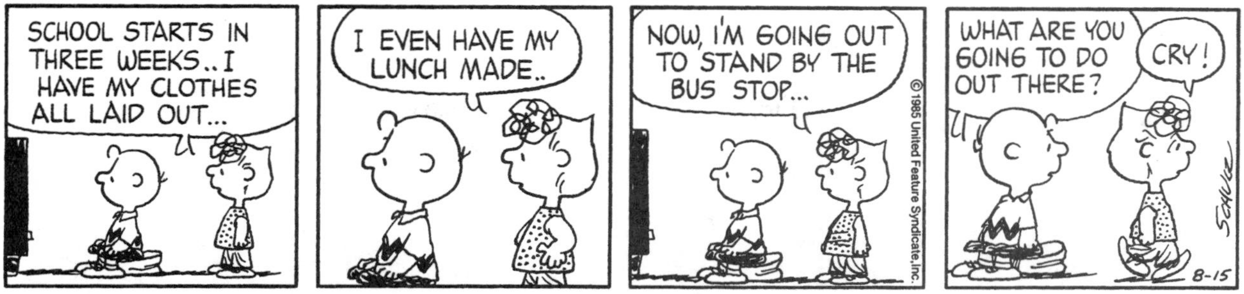
SCHOOL STARTS IN THREE WEEKS.. I HAVE MY CLOTHES ALL LAID OUT...
I EVEN HAVE MY LUNCH MADE..
NOW, I'M GOING OUT TO STAND BY THE BUS STOP...
© 1985 United Feature Syndicate, Inc.
WHAT ARE YOU GOING TO DO OUT THERE?
CRY!
8-15

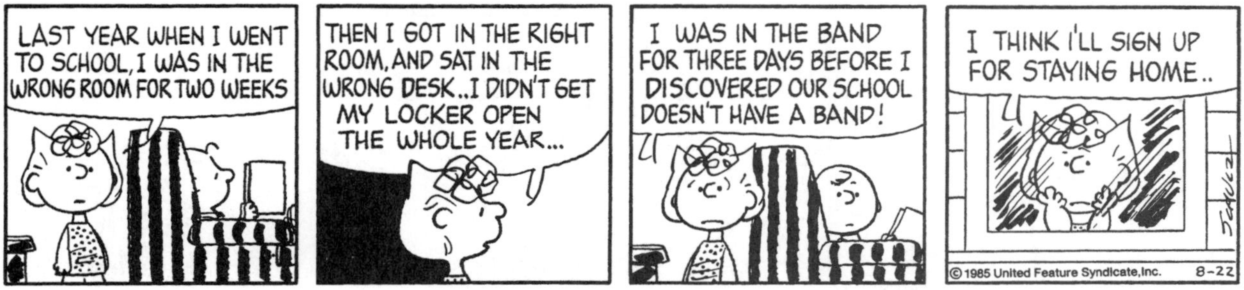
LAST YEAR WHEN I WENT TO SCHOOL, I WAS IN THE WRONG ROOM FOR TWO WEEKS
THEN I GOT IN THE RIGHT ROOM, AND SAT IN THE WRONG DESK.. I DIDN'T GET MY LOCKER OPEN THE WHOLE YEAR...
I WAS IN THE BAND FOR THREE DAYS BEFORE I DISCOVERED OUR SCHOOL DOESN'T HAVE A BAND!
I THINK I'LL SIGN UP FOR STAYING HOME..
© 1985 United Feature Syndicate, Inc.
8-22

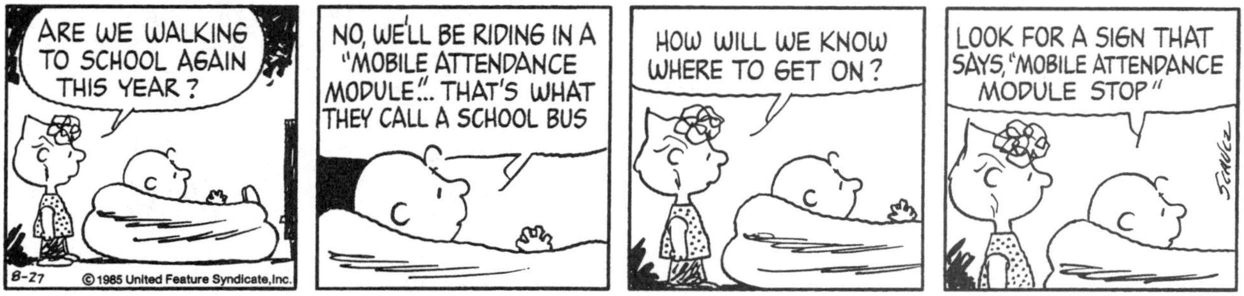
ARE WE WALKING TO SCHOOL AGAIN THIS YEAR?
8-27
© 1985 United Feature Syndicate, Inc.
NO, WE'LL BE RIDING IN A "MOBILE ATTENDANCE MODULE".. THAT'S WHAT THEY CALL A SCHOOL BUS
HOW WILL WE KNOW WHERE TO GET ON?
LOOK FOR A SIGN THAT SAYS, "MOBILE ATTENDANCE MODULE STOP"

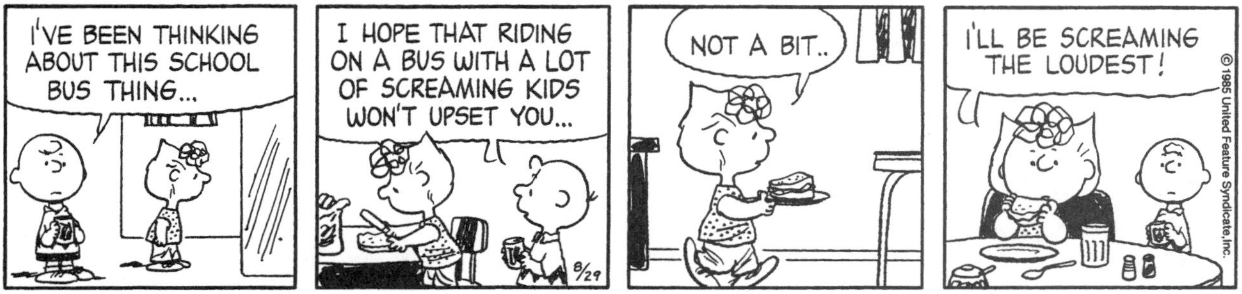
I'VE BEEN THINKING ABOUT THIS SCHOOL BUS THING...
I HOPE THAT RIDING ON A BUS WITH A LOT OF SCREAMING KIDS WON'T UPSET YOU...
8/29
NOT A BIT..
I'LL BE SCREAMING THE LOUDEST!
© 1985 United Feature Syndicate, Inc.

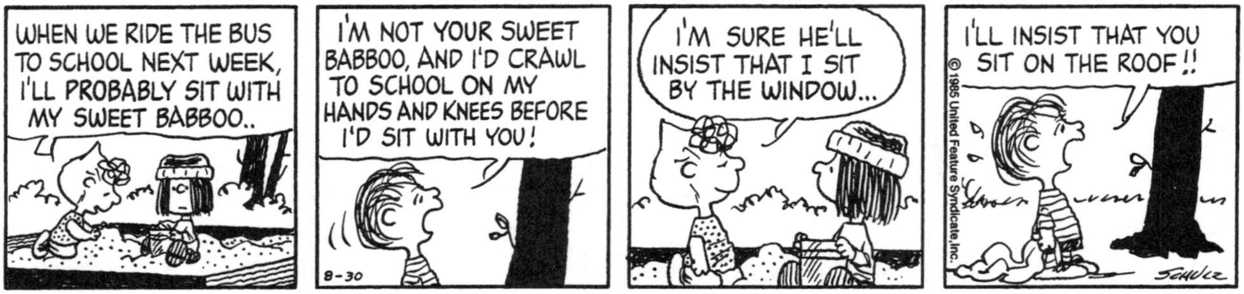
WHEN WE RIDE THE BUS TO SCHOOL NEXT WEEK, I'LL PROBABLY SIT WITH MY SWEET BABBOO..
I'M NOT YOUR SWEET BABBOO, AND I'D CRAWL TO SCHOOL ON MY HANDS AND KNEES BEFORE I'D SIT WITH YOU!
8-30
I'M SURE HE'LL INSIST THAT I SIT BY THE WINDOW...
© 1985 United Feature Syndicate, Inc.
I'LL INSIST THAT YOU SIT ON THE ROOF!!

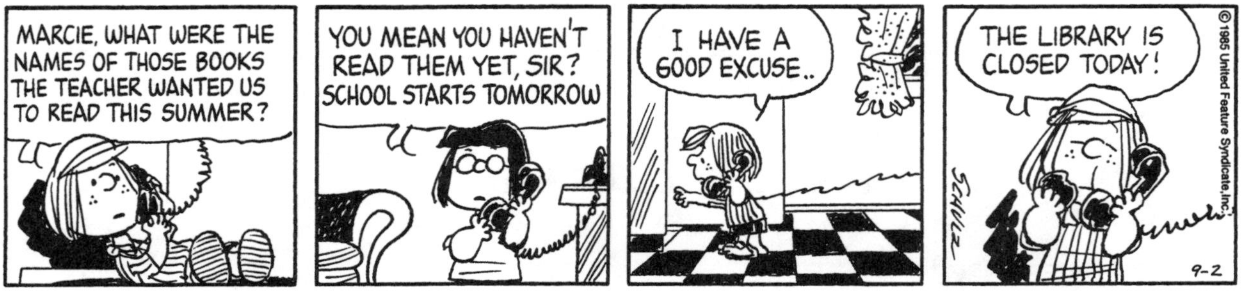
MARCIE, WHAT WERE THE NAMES OF THOSE BOOKS THE TEACHER WANTED US TO READ THIS SUMMER?
YOU MEAN YOU HAVEN'T READ THEM YET, SIR? SCHOOL STARTS TOMORROW
I HAVE A GOOD EXCUSE..
THE LIBRARY IS CLOSED TODAY!
© 1985 United Feature Syndicate, Inc.
9-2

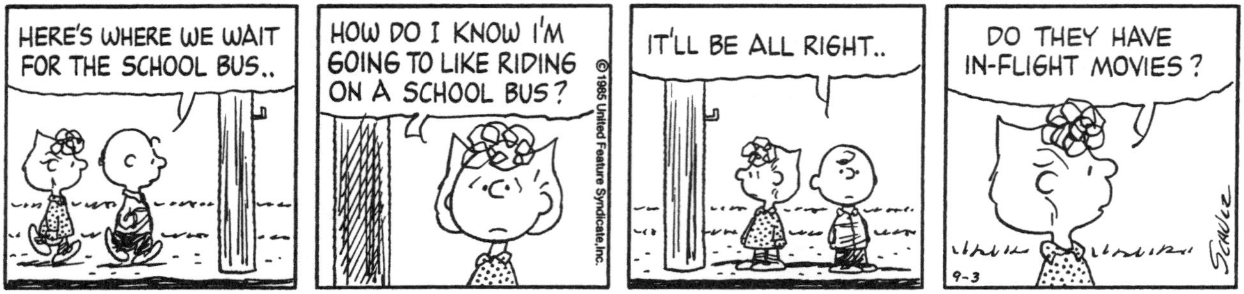
HERE'S WHERE WE WAIT FOR THE SCHOOL BUS..
HOW DO I KNOW I'M GOING TO LIKE RIDING ON A SCHOOL BUS?
© 1985 United Feature Syndicate, Inc.
IT'LL BE ALL RIGHT..
DO THEY HAVE IN-FLIGHT MOVIES?
9-3

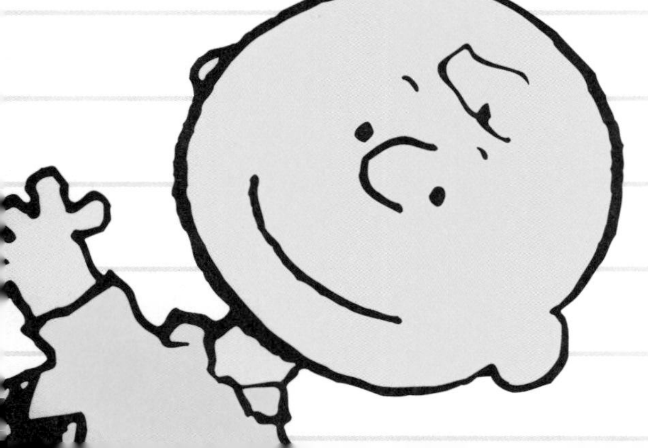

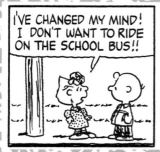

I'VE CHANGED MY MIND! I DON'T WANT TO RIDE ON THE SCHOOL BUS!!
I'LL GET CLAUSTROPHOBIA! I CAN'T DO IT! I CAN'T!!
© 1985 United Feature Syndicate, Inc.
WELL, LET'S JUST WALK THEN.. WE HAVE PLENTY OF TIME...
THANK YOU FOR BEING SO UNDERSTANDING, BIG BROTHER..
I DIDN'T WANT TO RIDE ON THE BUS EITHER!

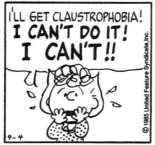

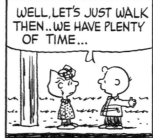

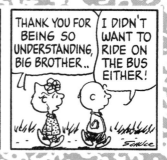

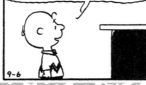

NO, MA'AM, MY SISTER AND I DIDN'T RIDE THE SCHOOL BUS THIS MORNING.. NO, MA'AM, WE WALKED...
THE COMPUTER SAID WE WERE ON THE BUS? NO, MA'AM, WE WALKED..
NO, MA'AM, WE NEVER GOT OFF THE BUS BECAUSE WE WERE NEVER ON THE BUS.. WE WALKED...
© 1985 United Feature Syndicate, Inc.
NO, MA'AM.. I NEVER KNOW WHAT'S GOING ON, EITHER.. I JUST SIT HERE

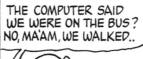

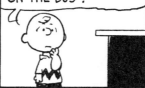

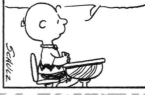

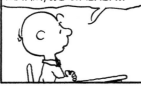

YES, SIR, MR. PRINCIPAL.. I WAS TOLD TO COME SEE YOU... YES, I'M IN SCHOOL TODAY...
THE COMPUTER SAID I WAS ON THE BUS? AND I NEVER GOT OFF? MY SISTER AND I WALKED, SIR
© 1985 United Feature Syndicate, Inc.
IT WAS A NICE MORNING SO WE WALKED.. THE COMPUTER SAID WE WERE ON THE BUS?
NO, SIR, I'M NOT A TROUBLEMAKER

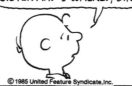

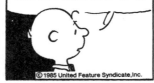

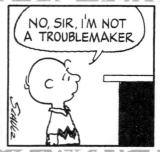

HEY, CHUCK, I HEARD THEM TALKING ABOUT YOU AT SCHOOL YESTERDAY...
THE COMPUTER SAID YOU WERE SUPPOSED TO BE ON OUR SCHOOL BUS...
© 1985 United Feature Syndicate, Inc.
THAT'S RIDICULOUS! I DON'T EVEN GO TO YOUR SCHOOL!!
WHAT ARE YOU, CHUCK, SOME KIND OF TROUBLEMAKER?
9-7
SCHULZ

HERE COMES THE SCHOOL BUS
© 1985 United Feature Syndicate, Inc.
THE DRIVER SAYS HE CAN'T TAKE YOU..YOUR NAME ISN'T ON THE COMPUTER LIST...
TELL HIM I'M YOUR BROTHER!
9-9
HE WANTS TO KNOW IF YOU'RE SOME KIND OF TROUBLEMAKER..
SCHULZ

YES, MA'AM..I'M LATE...I DIDN'T PLAN TO BE LATE...
9-10
THE BUS DRIVER SAID I WASN'T ON HIS COMPUTER LIST SO I HAD TO WALK...
© 1985 United Feature Syndicate, Inc.
I ALSO FORGOT MY LUNCH AND MY HOMEWORK, AND I'M PROBABLY SITTING IN THE WRONG DESK..
HOW DID I KNOW THAT?
SCHULZ

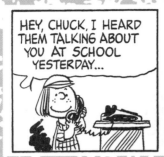

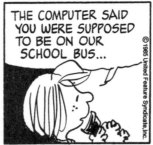

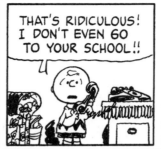

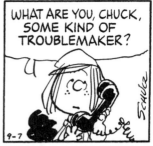

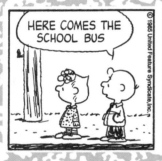

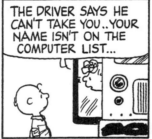

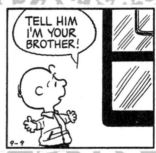

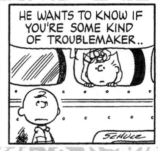

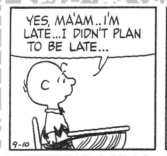

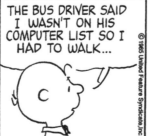

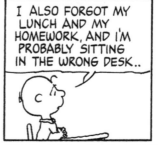

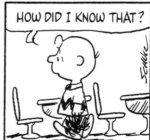

"WHAT MADE THIS COUNTRY GREAT?"
© 1986 United Feature Syndicate, Inc.
1-13
WHAT DID YOU PUT DOWN FOR THAT QUESTION, MARCIE?
"FAITH, COURAGE AND HARD WORK"... WHAT DID YOU PUT DOWN?
"PEANUT BUTTER SANDWICHES"

I HAVE TO WRITE A REPORT FOR SCHOOL ON THE SECRET OF LIFE...
CAN YOU GIVE ME SOME SUGGESTIONS?
© 1986 United Feature Syndicate, Inc.
4-2
TURN OFF APPLIANCES WHEN NOT IN USE, FORM CAR POOLS AND DEFROST FOODS BEFORE COOKING
I'LL GO ASK SOMEONE ELSE

SCHOOL STARTS NEXT WEEK..I HOPE I GET BETTER GRADES THIS YEAR
I HOPE I'LL BE THE PRETTIEST AND SMARTEST GIRL IN THE WHOLE CLASS..
© 1986 United Feature Syndicate, Inc.
"HOPE IS A GOOD BREAKFAST, BUT IT IS A BAD SUPPER"
8-27
WHEN WE GO TO COLLEGE, MARCIE, I'M NOT GOING TO ROOM WITH YOU..

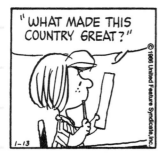

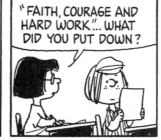

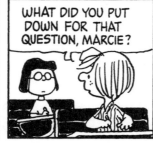

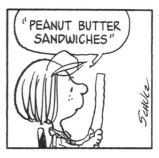

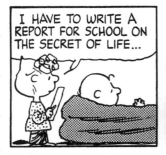

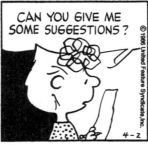

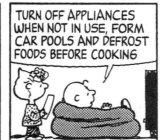

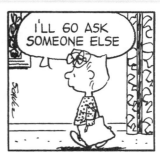

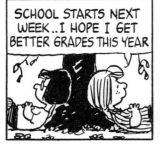

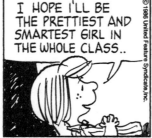

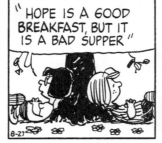

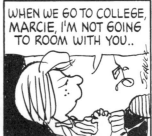

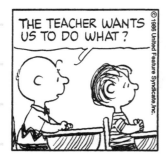

THE TEACHER WANTS US TO DO WHAT?
© 1986 United Feature Syndicate, Inc.
WALK UP TO THE FRONT OF THE ROOM, AND INTRODUCE OURSELVES.. WE ALWAYS DO IT ON THE FIRST DAY OF SCHOOL...
IT'S TOO FAR..
TOO FAR?
IT'S THIRTY MILES FROM MY DESK TO THE FRONT OF THE ROOM

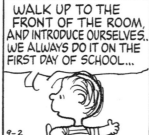

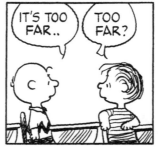

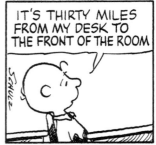

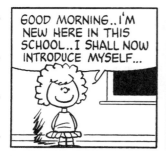

GOOD MORNING..I'M NEW HERE IN THIS SCHOOL..I SHALL NOW INTRODUCE MYSELF...
MY NAME IS TAPIOCA PUDDING
WITH MY NAME, MY BLOND HAIR AND MY SMILE, MY DAD SAYS WE CAN MAKE A MILLION DOLLARS..
© 1986 United Feature Syndicate, Inc.
MY DAD IS IN LICENSING!

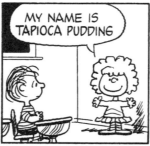

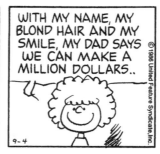

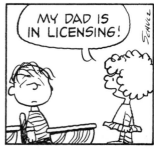

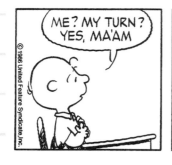

© 1986 United Feature Syndicate, Inc.
ME? MY TURN? YES, MA'AM
MY NAME IS CHARLES BROWN..MY DAD IS A BARBER...I GUESS MY FAVORITE HOBBIES ARE BASEBALL AND READING
I THOUGHT I DID PRETTY GOOD..WHY DID EVERYONE LAUGH?
YOU WALKED OUT THE DOOR, AND GAVE YOUR SPEECH IN THE HALLWAY!

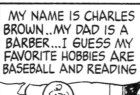

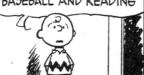

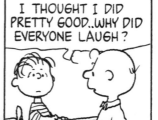

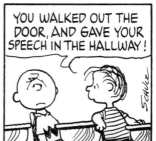

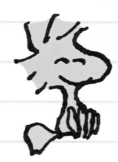

EXCUSE ME..WHAT DID YOU SAY YOUR NAME IS?

TAPIOCA PUDDING... MY DAD GAVE ME MY NAME.. HE'S IN LICENSING...

© 1986 United Feature Syndicate, Inc.

9-5

HE SAID I'M GOING TO BE ON GREETING CARDS, LUNCH BOXES, TV AND EVERYTHING!

BUT, OBVIOUSLY, NO BEER COMMERCIALS.. OBVIOUSLY

YOU SEE, MY DAD'S NAME IS JOE PUDDING SO IT WAS ONLY NATURAL THAT I'D BE CALLED TAPIOCA PUDDING..

MY DAD'S IN LICENSING, YOU KNOW

I KNOW

© 1986 United Feature Syndicate, Inc.

WITH MY NAME AND FACE ON EVERY GREETING CARD AND CEREAL BOX IN THE COUNTRY, MY DAD SAYS WE'LL MAKE A MILLION..

9-9

YOU DON'T KNOW ANYTHING ABOUT INVESTMENTS, DO YOU?

I'M SO EXCITED! I THINK I'VE FOUND AN AGENT!

I'M MEETING HIM RIGHT AFTER SCHOOL TODAY.. HERE'S THE CARD HE SENT ME...

© 1986 United Feature Syndicate, Inc.

9-15

"ACE LICENSING.". SOUNDS IMPRESSIVE...

HERE'S THE WORLD FAMOUS AGENT ON HIS WAY TO SIGN UP ANOTHER CLIENT..

"TO DIVIDE FRACTIONS, USE THE RECIPROCAL AND MULTIPLY"
© 1986 United Feature Syndicate, Inc.
9-22
WHY?
WHY USE THE RECIPROCAL?
NO, WHY WAS I BORN?
SCHULZ

YES, MA'AM.. A REPORT ON THE FRENCH REVOLUTION..
© 1986 United Feature Syndicate, Inc.
TWO THOUSAND WORDS?
9-24
YES, MA'AM
PLEASE ALLOW FOUR TO SIX WEEKS FOR DELIVERY
SCHULZ

THIS IS THE POEM I HAVE MEMORIZED..
10-22
"FOG" BY CARL SANDBURG
© 1986 United Feature Syndicate, Inc.
OKAY! START THE POTS!
JUST A LITTLE SPECIAL EFFECT, MA'AM..
SCHULZ

8-22
WHAT ARE YOU DOING HERE?
I'M PRACTICING WAITING FOR THE SCHOOL BUS..
IS THAT SOMETHING YOU HAVE TO PRACTICE?
IT IS IF YOU WANT TO BE GOOD AT IT..
SCHULZ
© 1987 United Feature Syndicate, Inc.

© 1987 United Feature Syndicate, Inc.
RIGHT HERE, NEXT WEEK
9-3
THIS IS THE SPOT WHERE THE SCHOOL BUS WILL BE STOPPING...
I'LL BE OVER HERE..
THIS IS THE POLE I'M GOING TO CHAIN MYSELF TO..
SCHULZ

© 1987 United Feature Syndicate, Inc.
ME?
9-28
NO, MA'AM, I WASN'T GIVING THE ANSWERS...
I WAS JUST LEAKING INFORMATION..
SCHULZ

WE'RE HAVING A TEST TOMORROW IN SCHOOL... ASK ME THESE QUESTIONS..
WHAT'S THE TALLEST MOUNTAIN IN THE WORLD?
WHO CARES?
WHAT'S THE LONGEST RIVER IN NORTH AMERICA?
WHO CARES?
© 1988 United Feature Syndicate, Inc.
YOU'RE EITHER READY OR YOU'RE NOT READY.. I DON'T KNOW WHICH..
WHO CARES?

IT WAS A VERY STIRRING SPEECH..
WHEN HE WAS THROUGH, THEY GAVE HIM A STANDING INVITATION!
OVATION
© 1988 United Feature Syndicate, Inc.
THEY SAID HE COULD STOP BY ANY TIME!

PEANUTS
WE GOT OUR TESTS BACK...
I WONDER WHAT GRADE I GOT... I HATE TO LOOK...
Tm. Reg. U. S. Pat. Off.—All rights reserved © 1973 by United Feature Syndicate, Inc.
"Z MINUS"?!!

" DEAR STUDENT, AS PART OF A STATEWIDE SCHOOL PROJECT, WE ARE ASKING WHAT YOU ARE READING NOW "
© 1988 United Feature Syndicate, Inc.
5-21
Right now, I am reading your form letter.
SCHULZ

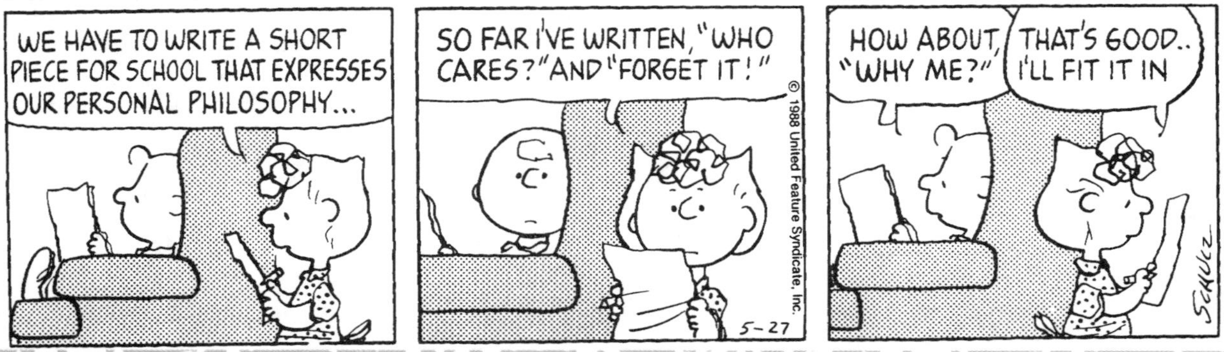
WE HAVE TO WRITE A SHORT PIECE FOR SCHOOL THAT EXPRESSES OUR PERSONAL PHILOSOPHY...
SO FAR I'VE WRITTEN, "WHO CARES?" AND "FORGET IT!"
© 1988 United Feature Syndicate, Inc.
5-27
HOW ABOUT, "WHY ME?"
THAT'S GOOD.. I'LL FIT IT IN
SCHULZ

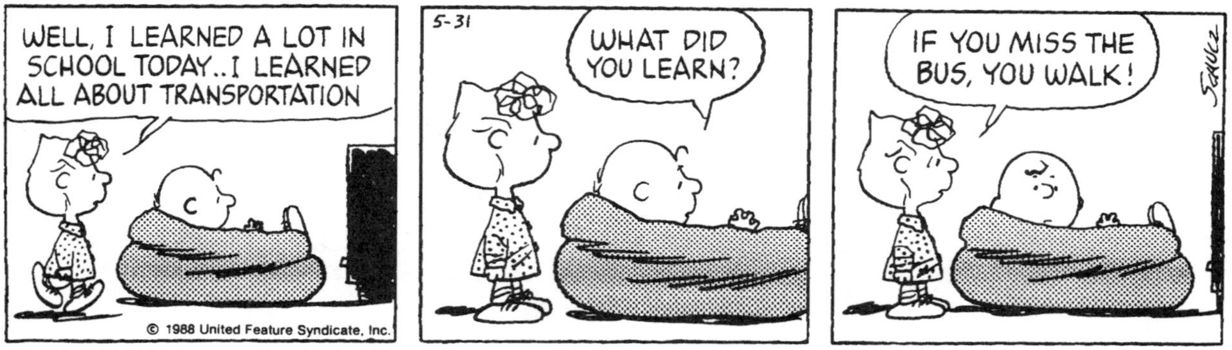
WELL, I LEARNED A LOT IN SCHOOL TODAY..I LEARNED ALL ABOUT TRANSPORTATION
© 1988 United Feature Syndicate, Inc.
5-31
WHAT DID YOU LEARN?
IF YOU MISS THE BUS, YOU WALK!
SCHULZ

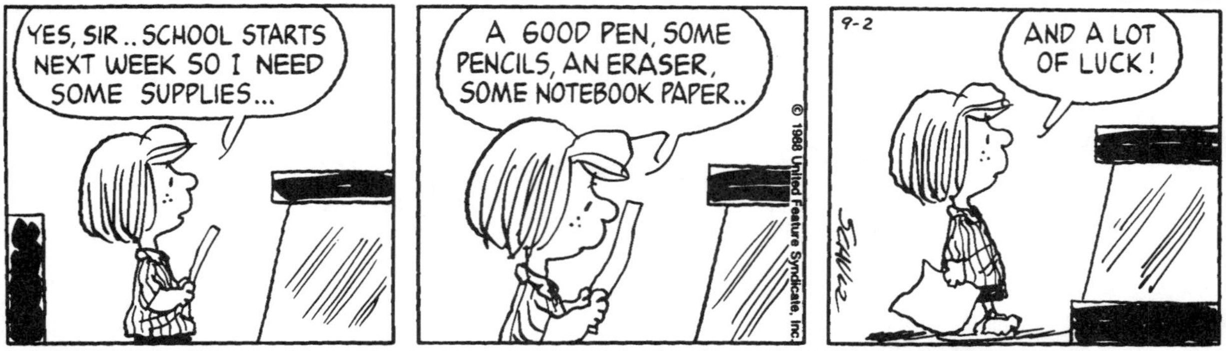
YES, SIR..SCHOOL STARTS NEXT WEEK SO I NEED SOME SUPPLIES...
A GOOD PEN, SOME PENCILS, AN ERASER, SOME NOTEBOOK PAPER..
© 1988 United Feature Syndicate, Inc.
9-2
AND A LOT OF LUCK!
SCHULZ

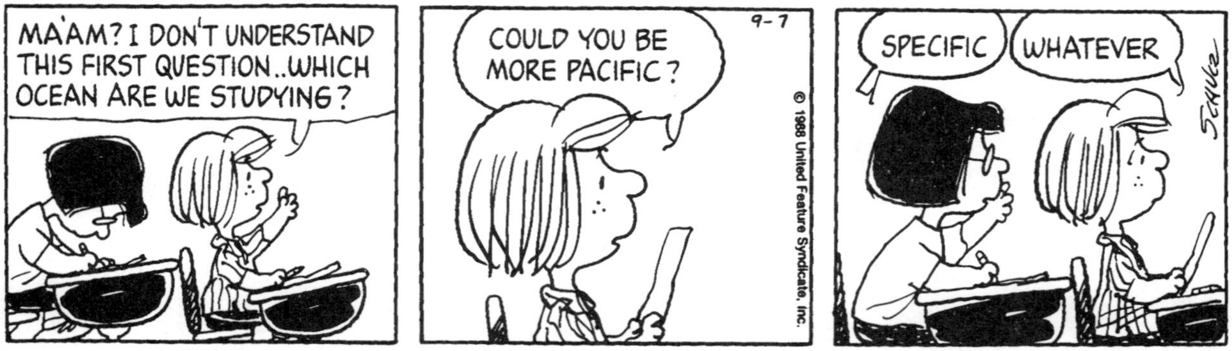
MA'AM? I DON'T UNDERSTAND THIS FIRST QUESTION..WHICH OCEAN ARE WE STUDYING?
9-7
COULD YOU BE MORE PACIFIC?
© 1988 United Feature Syndicate, Inc.
SPECIFIC
WHATEVER
SCHULZ

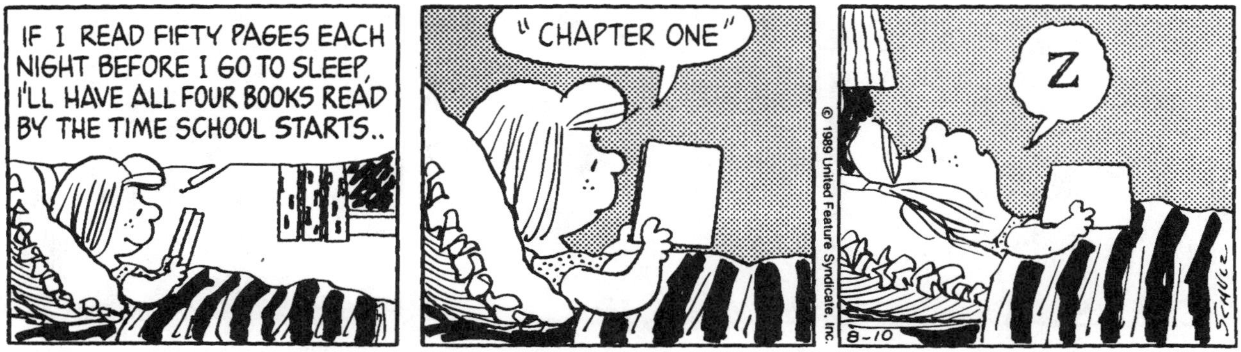
IF I READ FIFTY PAGES EACH NIGHT BEFORE I GO TO SLEEP, I'LL HAVE ALL FOUR BOOKS READ BY THE TIME SCHOOL STARTS..
"CHAPTER ONE"
© 1989 United Feature Syndicate, Inc.
Z
8-10
SCHULZ

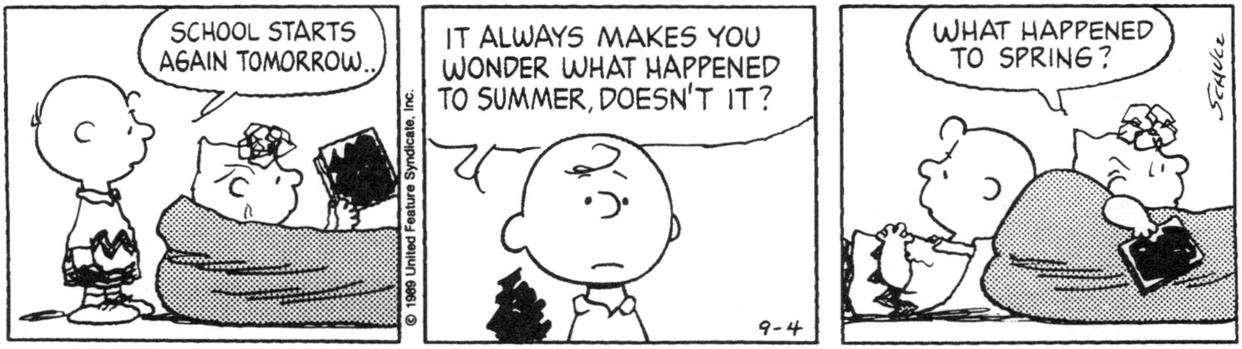
SCHOOL STARTS AGAIN TOMORROW..
© 1989 United Feature Syndicate, Inc.
IT ALWAYS MAKES YOU WONDER WHAT HAPPENED TO SUMMER, DOESN'T IT?
9-4
WHAT HAPPENED TO SPRING?
SCHULZ

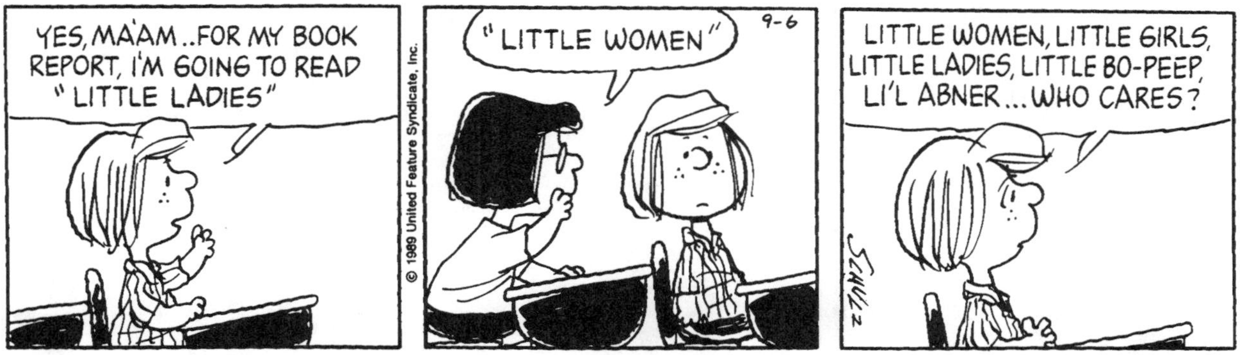
YES, MA'AM..FOR MY BOOK REPORT, I'M GOING TO READ "LITTLE LADIES"
© 1989 United Feature Syndicate, Inc.
"LITTLE WOMEN"
9-6
LITTLE WOMEN, LITTLE GIRLS, LITTLE LADIES, LITTLE BO-PEEP, LI'L ABNER... WHO CARES?
SCHULZ

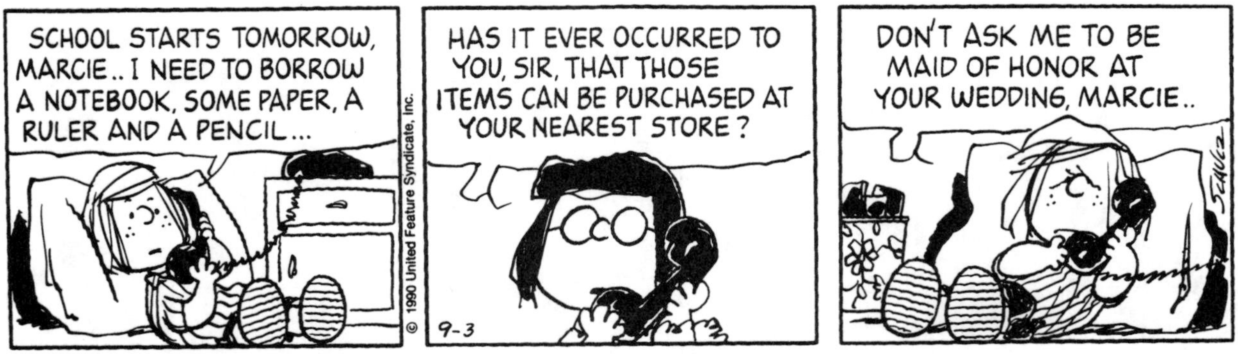
SCHOOL STARTS TOMORROW, MARCIE.. I NEED TO BORROW A NOTEBOOK, SOME PAPER, A RULER AND A PENCIL...
HAS IT EVER OCCURRED TO YOU, SIR, THAT THOSE ITEMS CAN BE PURCHASED AT YOUR NEAREST STORE?
9-3
DON'T ASK ME TO BE MAID OF HONOR AT YOUR WEDDING, MARCIE..
SCHULZ

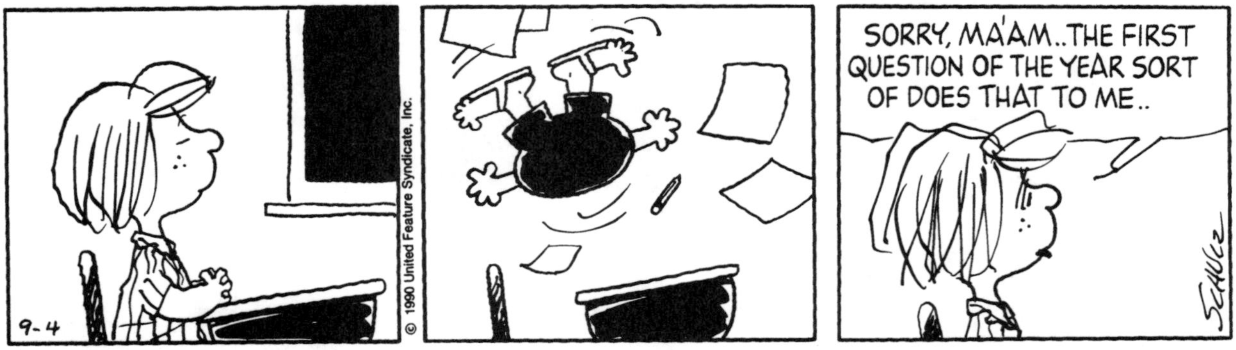
9-4
SORRY, MA'AM..THE FIRST QUESTION OF THE YEAR SORT OF DOES THAT TO ME..
SCHULZ

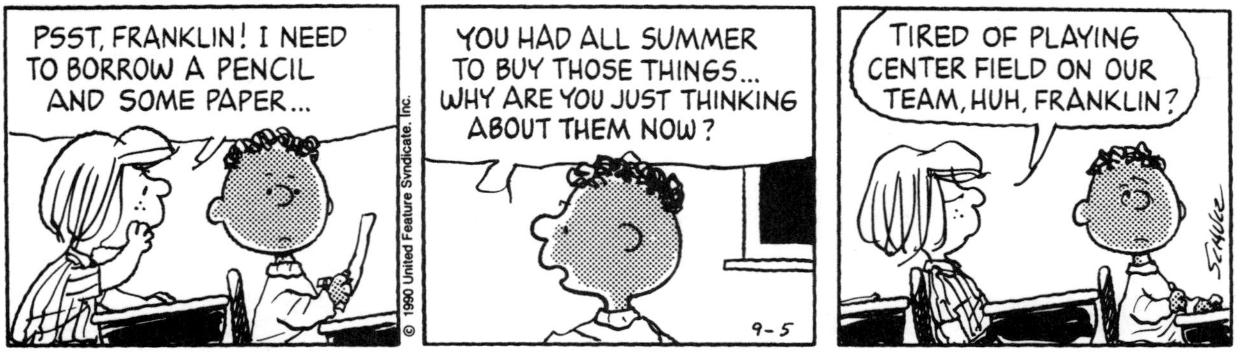
PSST, FRANKLIN! I NEED TO BORROW A PENCIL AND SOME PAPER...
YOU HAD ALL SUMMER TO BUY THOSE THINGS... WHY ARE YOU JUST THINKING ABOUT THEM NOW?
9-5
TIRED OF PLAYING CENTER FIELD ON OUR TEAM, HUH, FRANKLIN?
SCHULZ

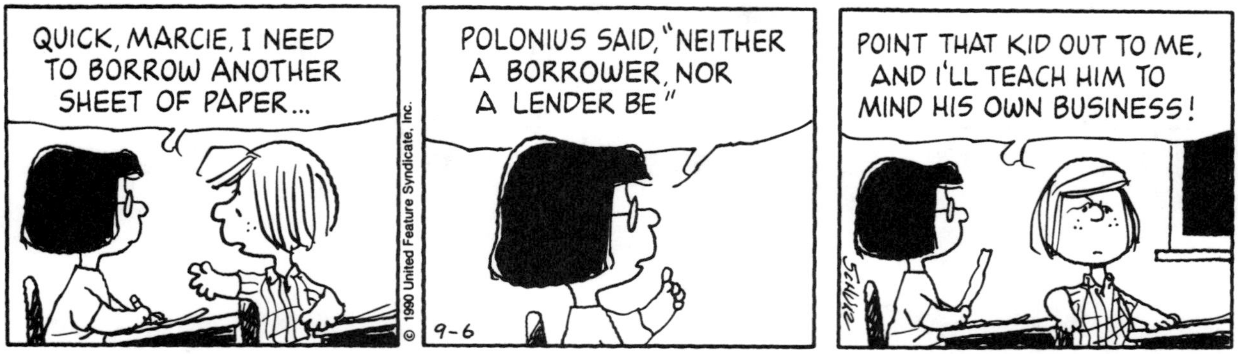
QUICK, MARCIE, I NEED TO BORROW ANOTHER SHEET OF PAPER...
POLONIUS SAID, "NEITHER A BORROWER, NOR A LENDER BE"
9-6
POINT THAT KID OUT TO ME, AND I'LL TEACH HIM TO MIND HIS OWN BUSINESS!
SCHULZ

11-5
WHAT DID YOU LEARN IN SCHOOL TODAY?
© 1990 United Feature Syndicate, Inc.
THE DOOR INTO THE SCHOOL BUS HAS THREE STEPS, AND THE HANDLE ON THE DRINKING FOUNTAIN IS ON THE RIGHT...
AND EVERYBODY TOLD ME THAT SECOND GRADE WAS GOING TO BE SO HARD!
SCHULZ

WE STUDIED EXCLAMATION POINTS IN SCHOOL TODAY..
© 1991 United Feature Syndicate, Inc.
! ! ! ! ! ! ! ! ! ! ! ! ! ! !
THEY LOOK VERY GOOD!!!!
THANK YOU!!!!!!
SCHULZ
4-24

SCHOOL STARTS AGAIN NEXT WEEK, DOESN'T IT?
THAT'S RIGHT
© 1991 United Feature Syndicate, Inc.
8-26
WHEE!
SCHULZ

YES, SIR .. I NEED SOME SCHOOL SUPPLIES...
SOME PENCILS, SOME PAPER, A LOOSE-LEAF BINDER...
..AND SOME ANSWERS.. I NEED A LOT OF ANSWERS..
© 1991 United Feature Syndicate, Inc.
8-27

SCHOOL STARTS TOMORROW!!
GO BACK TO SLEEP..
© 1991 United Feature Syndicate, Inc.
9-2

HAS THE SCHOOL BUS COME YET?
NOT YET
TELL ME WHEN IT COMES
I WILL
I DIDN'T DO MY HOMEWORK... THE TEACHER'S GONNA KILL ME..
9-24
HAS THE BUS COME YET?
NOT YET
© 1991 United Feature Syndicate, Inc.
THEN I'M STILL ALIVE
SCHULZ

11-5
DID YOU GET THE FIRST PROBLEM, SIR?
© 1991 United Feature Syndicate, Inc.
WELL, IT'S FRACTIONS, ISN'T IT?
I PUT DOWN, "SIX OF ONE AND HALF A DOZEN OF THE OTHER"
SCHULZ

YES, MA'AM..I NEED TO EXPLAIN SOMETHING ABOUT MY REPORT..
11-20
WELL, MY DOG SORT OF GOT HOLD OF IT..
© 1991 United Feature Syndicate, Inc.
OH, NO, MA'AM.. HE DIDN'T CHEW IT UP..
SCHULZ
ACTUALLY, HE WROTE IT!

YES, MA'AM .. "A TALE OF TWO CITIES"
© 1992 United Feature Syndicate, Inc.
CHARLIE DICKENS
CHUCK ? CHAZ ? CHARLES ? WHATEVER ..

THIS IS MY REPORT ON "A TALE OF TWO CITIES" BY CHARLES DICKENS ..
2-12
© 1992 United Feature Syndicate, Inc.
"ST. PAUL AND MINNEAPOLIS ARE ..."
ONE OF THE GREAT TRIES OF ALL TIME, SIR

PEANUTS
by SCHULZ
SCHOOL STARTS TOMORROW!
GOOD GRIEF!
GET ALL YOUR SCHOOL CLOTHES READY!
9-6
© 1992 United Feature Syndicate, Inc.
EAT A GOOD BREAKFAST!! SCHOOL STARTS TOMORROW!
GET THOSE BOOKS READY! SHARPEN THOSE PENCILS!
SCHULZ
WHAT ARE YOU DOING BACK IN BED? SCHOOL STARTS TOMORROW..
WHO CARES?

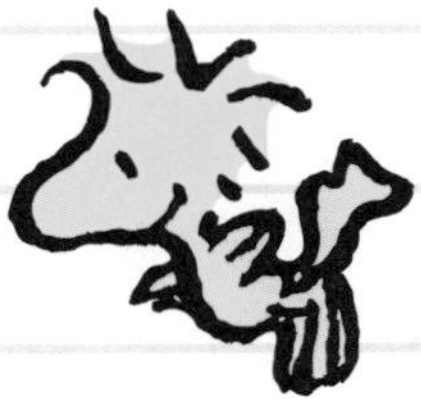

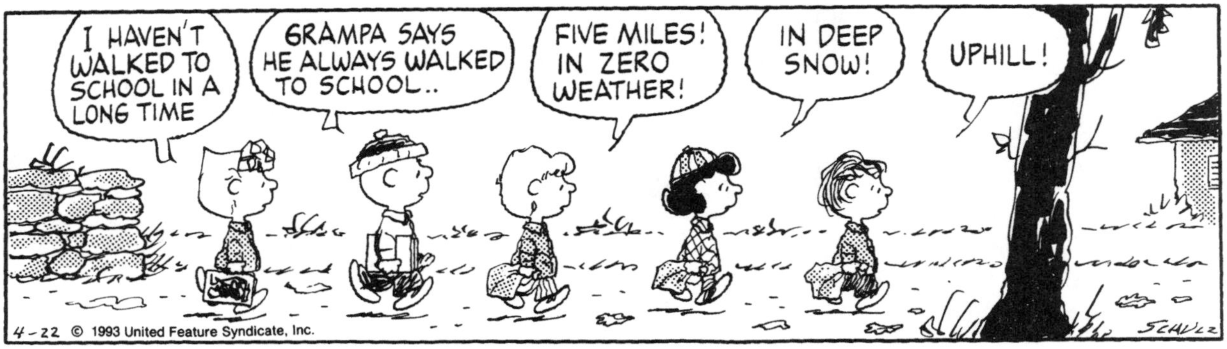

I HAVEN'T WALKED TO SCHOOL IN A LONG TIME
GRAMPA SAYS HE ALWAYS WALKED TO SCHOOL..
FIVE MILES! IN ZERO WEATHER!
IN DEEP SNOW!
UPHILL!
4-22 © 1993 United Feature Syndicate, Inc.
SCHULZ

SCHOOL STARTS IN FOUR WEEKS!!
© 1993 United Feature Syndicate, Inc.
DETAILS AT ELEVEN..
8-12
SCHULZ

YES, SIR.. WE'D LIKE TO BUY SOME SCHOOL SUPPLIES
THINGS LIKE PAPER AND PENCILS..
AND LOTS OF ERASERS..
© 1993 United Feature Syndicate, Inc.
8-13
SCHULZ

THIS IS MY REPORT ON HAMLET..

A HAMLET IS A SMALL VILLAGE WITH A POPULATION OF MAYBE A FEW HUNDRED, AND..

5-19

MA'AM?

FAR AND AWAY, SIR, ONE OF THE GREAT TRIES OF ALL TIME!

I CAN'T STAND IT..

© 1994 United Feature Syndicate, Inc.

SCHOOL STARTS NEXT WEEK.. I NEED YOU TO TEST ME ON MY MULTIPLICATION TABLES...
OKAY, HOW MUCH IS FIVE TIMES EIGHT?
WHO CARES?
I THINK YOU'RE READY
© 1993 United Feature Syndicate, Inc.
SCHULZ
9-1

SCHOOL STARTS TOMORROW!!
9-6
© 1993 United Feature Syndicate, Inc.
WOULD YOU RECOGNIZE THE PRINCIPAL IF YOU MET HIM ON THE STREET?! BE READY! BE READY!
SCHULZ

AFTER I GRADUATE FROM SCHOOL, WILL I BE A BETTER PERSON?
PROBABLY.. A GOOD EDUCATION IS VERY IMPORTANT
THAT'S RIGHT.. LEARNING ALWAYS MAKES YOU A BETTER PERSON..
UNLESS YOU DON'T HAVE A DOG..
9-7
SCHULZ
© 1993 United Feature Syndicate, Inc.

© 1993 United Feature Syndicate, Inc.
SCHOOL STARTED LAST WEEK!!
9-20
I WASN'T SURE YOU HAD NOTICED
SCHULZ

THIS IS THE BOOK I HAVE TO READ FOR SCHOOL..I WANT YOU TO READ IT FOR ME..
12-15
YOU MEAN I'M SUPPOSED TO READ IT WHILE YOU JUST SIT HERE AND LISTEN..
© 1993 United Feature Syndicate, Inc.
SCHULZ
LISTEN ?

SCHOOL STARTS TOMORROW!
SHARPEN THOSE PENCILS! READ THOSE BOOKS! MAKE THOSE LUNCHES!
DREAD THOSE MORNINGS!
© 1994 United Feature Syndicate, Inc.
9-6
SCHULZ

WHAT DID YOU PUT DOWN FOR THE THIRD QUESTION, SIR?
"WHERE IS ALBANIA?" I SAID IT'S RIGHT NEXT TO JOE BANIA..
© 1994 United Feature Syndicate, Inc.
10/25
PRETTY OBVIOUS, HUH, SIR?
VERY OBVIOUS..
SCHULZ

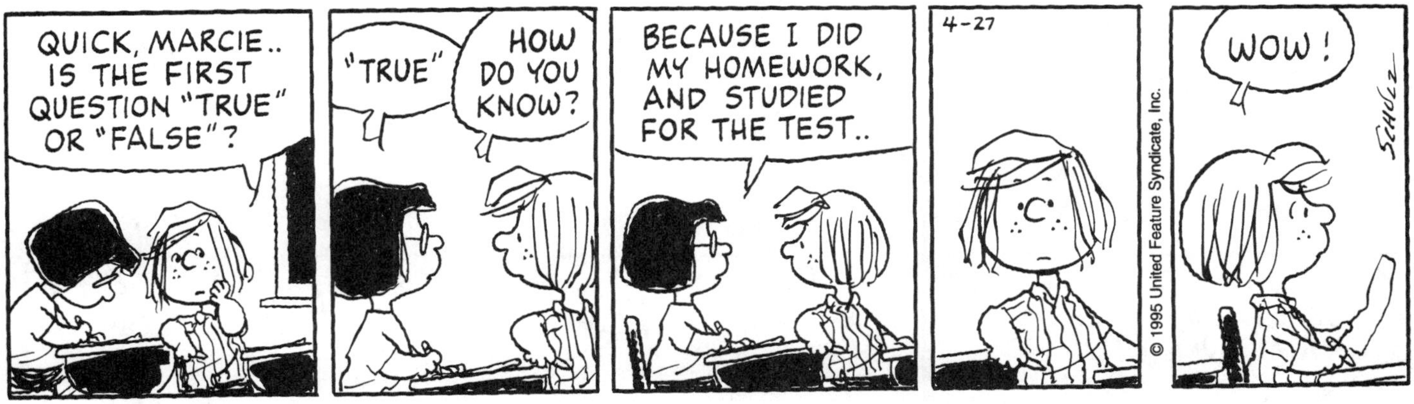
QUICK, MARCIE.. IS THE FIRST QUESTION "TRUE" OR "FALSE"?
"TRUE"
HOW DO YOU KNOW?
BECAUSE I DID MY HOMEWORK, AND STUDIED FOR THE TEST..
4-27
© 1995 United Feature Syndicate, Inc.
WOW!

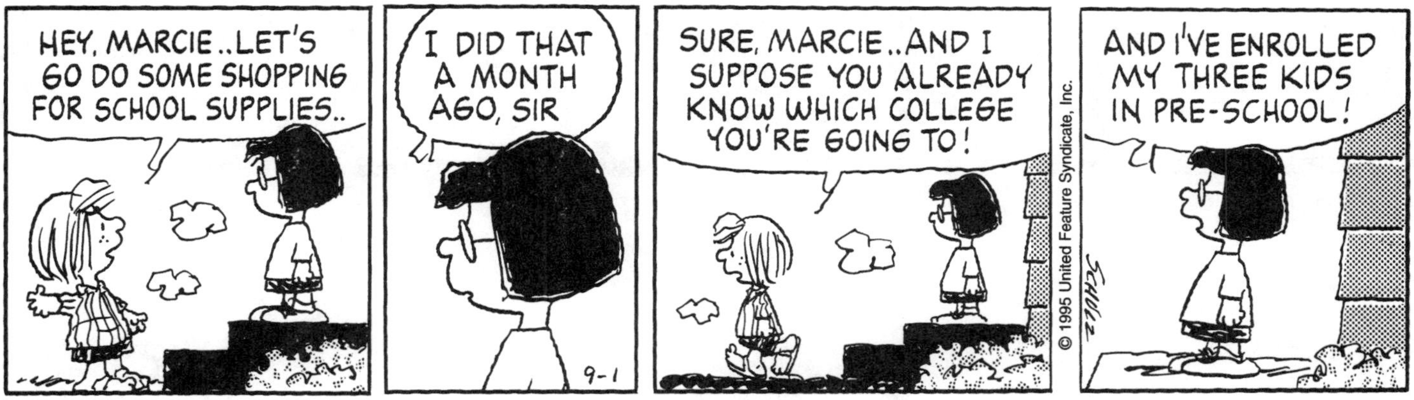
HEY, MARCIE..LET'S GO DO SOME SHOPPING FOR SCHOOL SUPPLIES..
I DID THAT A MONTH AGO, SIR
9-1
SURE, MARCIE..AND I SUPPOSE YOU ALREADY KNOW WHICH COLLEGE YOU'RE GOING TO!
© 1995 United Feature Syndicate, Inc.
AND I'VE ENROLLED MY THREE KIDS IN PRE-SCHOOL!

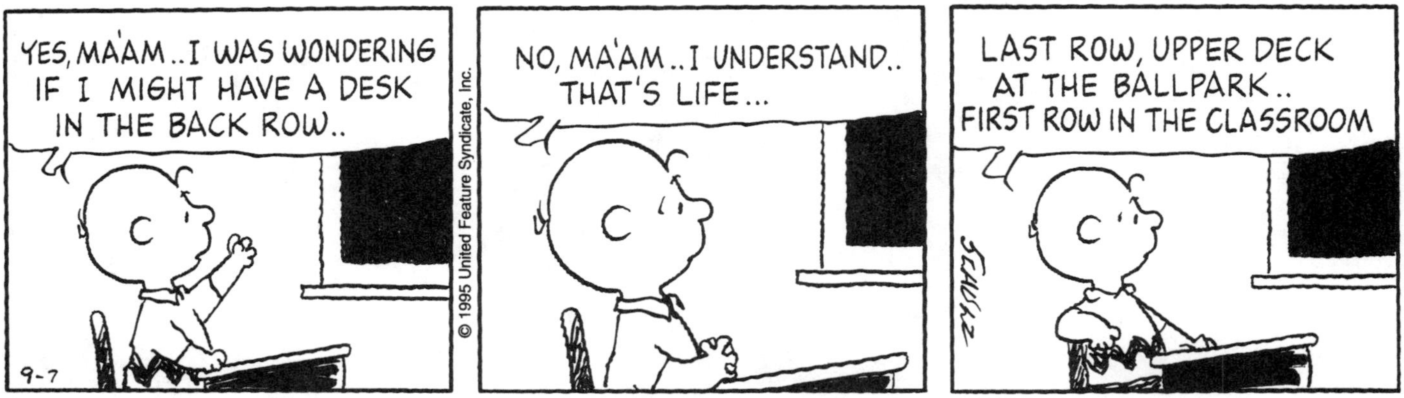
YES, MA'AM..I WAS WONDERING IF I MIGHT HAVE A DESK IN THE BACK ROW..
9-7
© 1995 United Feature Syndicate, Inc.
NO, MA'AM..I UNDERSTAND.. THAT'S LIFE...
LAST ROW, UPPER DECK AT THE BALLPARK.. FIRST ROW IN THE CLASSROOM

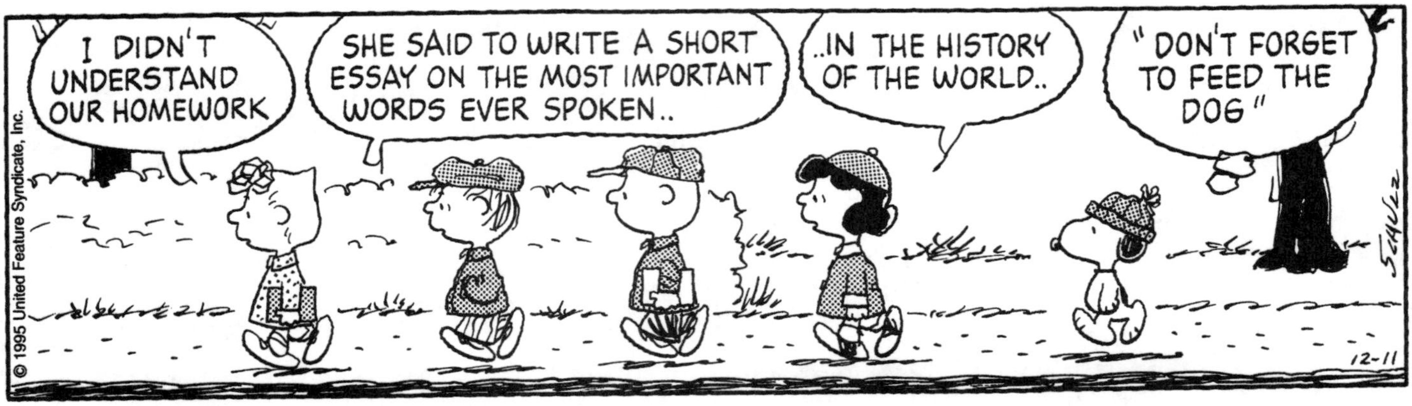
I DIDN'T UNDERSTAND OUR HOMEWORK
SHE SAID TO WRITE A SHORT ESSAY ON THE MOST IMPORTANT WORDS EVER SPOKEN..
..IN THE HISTORY OF THE WORLD..
"DON'T FORGET TO FEED THE DOG"
SCHULZ
12-11
© 1995 United Feature Syndicate, Inc.

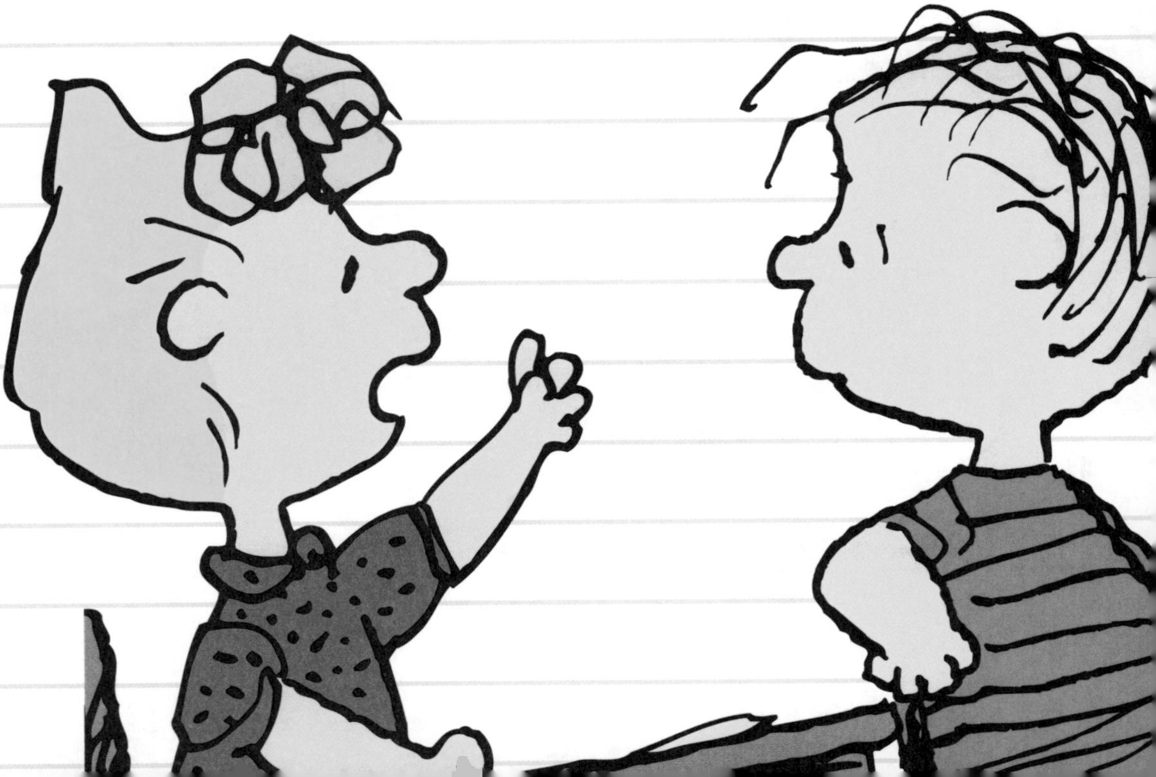

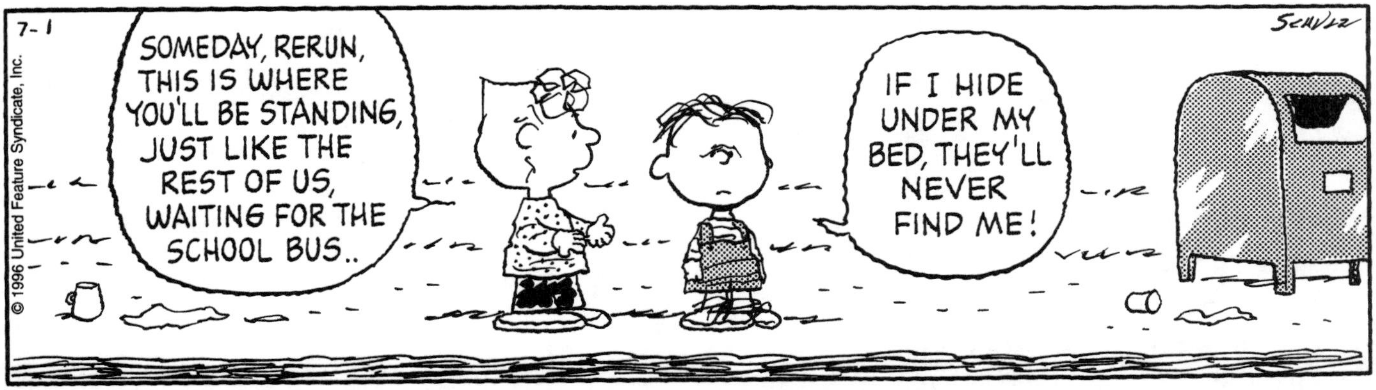
7-1
SCHULZ
© 1996 United Feature Syndicate, Inc.
SOMEDAY, RERUN, THIS IS WHERE YOU'LL BE STANDING, JUST LIKE THE REST OF US, WAITING FOR THE SCHOOL BUS..
IF I HIDE UNDER MY BED, THEY'LL NEVER FIND ME!

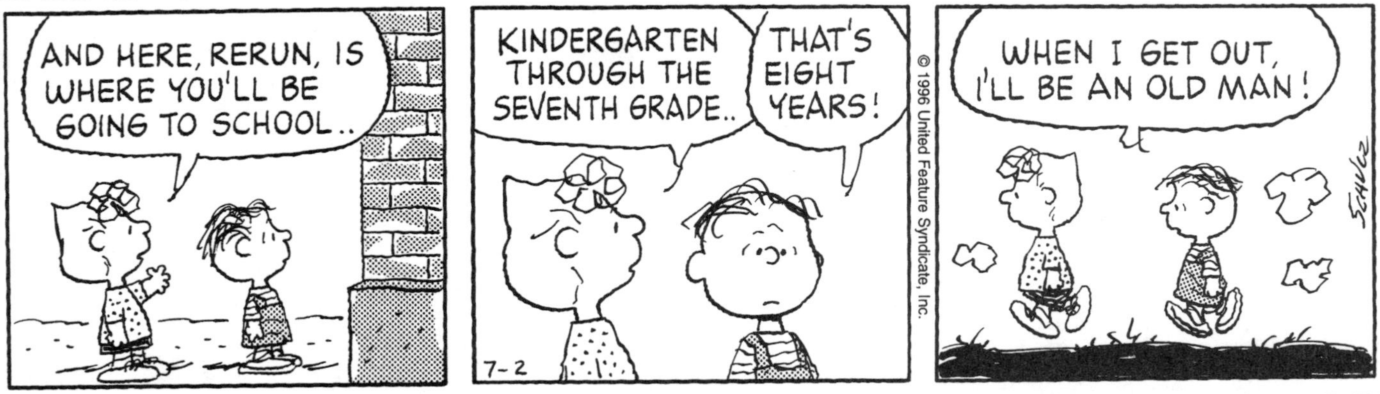
AND HERE, RERUN, IS WHERE YOU'LL BE GOING TO SCHOOL..
KINDERGARTEN THROUGH THE SEVENTH GRADE..
THAT'S EIGHT YEARS!
7-2
© 1996 United Feature Syndicate, Inc.
WHEN I GET OUT, I'LL BE AN OLD MAN!
SCHULZ

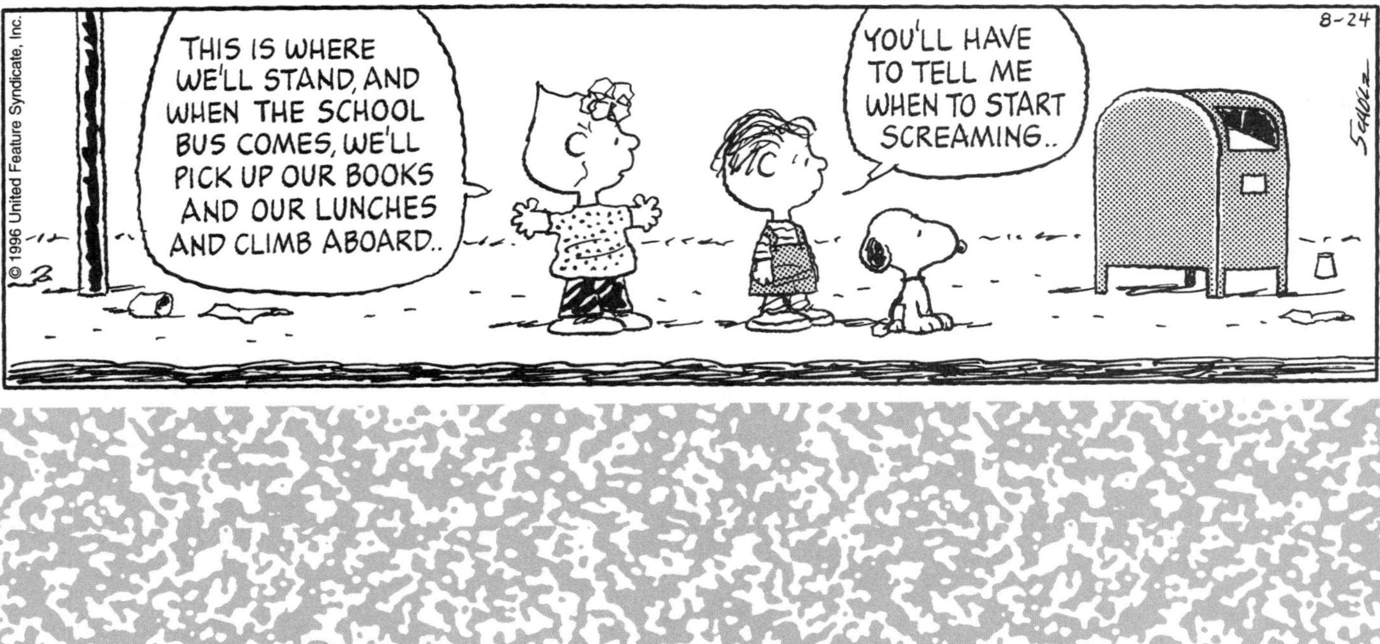
© 1996 United Feature Syndicate, Inc.
THIS IS WHERE WE'LL STAND, AND WHEN THE SCHOOL BUS COMES, WE'LL PICK UP OUR BOOKS AND OUR LUNCHES AND CLIMB ABOARD..
YOU'LL HAVE TO TELL ME WHEN TO START SCREAMING..
8-24
SCHULZ

WHY SHOULD I GO TO SCHOOL?
BECAUSE YOU CAN'T HIDE UNDER YOUR BED FOREVER!
THE GUARDS WILL HATE ME!
THEY DON'T HAVE GUARDS.. THEY'RE CALLED TEACHERS..
HOW WILL I GET ACROSS THE MOAT?
www.unitedmedia.com
© 1996 United Feature Syndicate, Inc.
9-4
SCHULZ

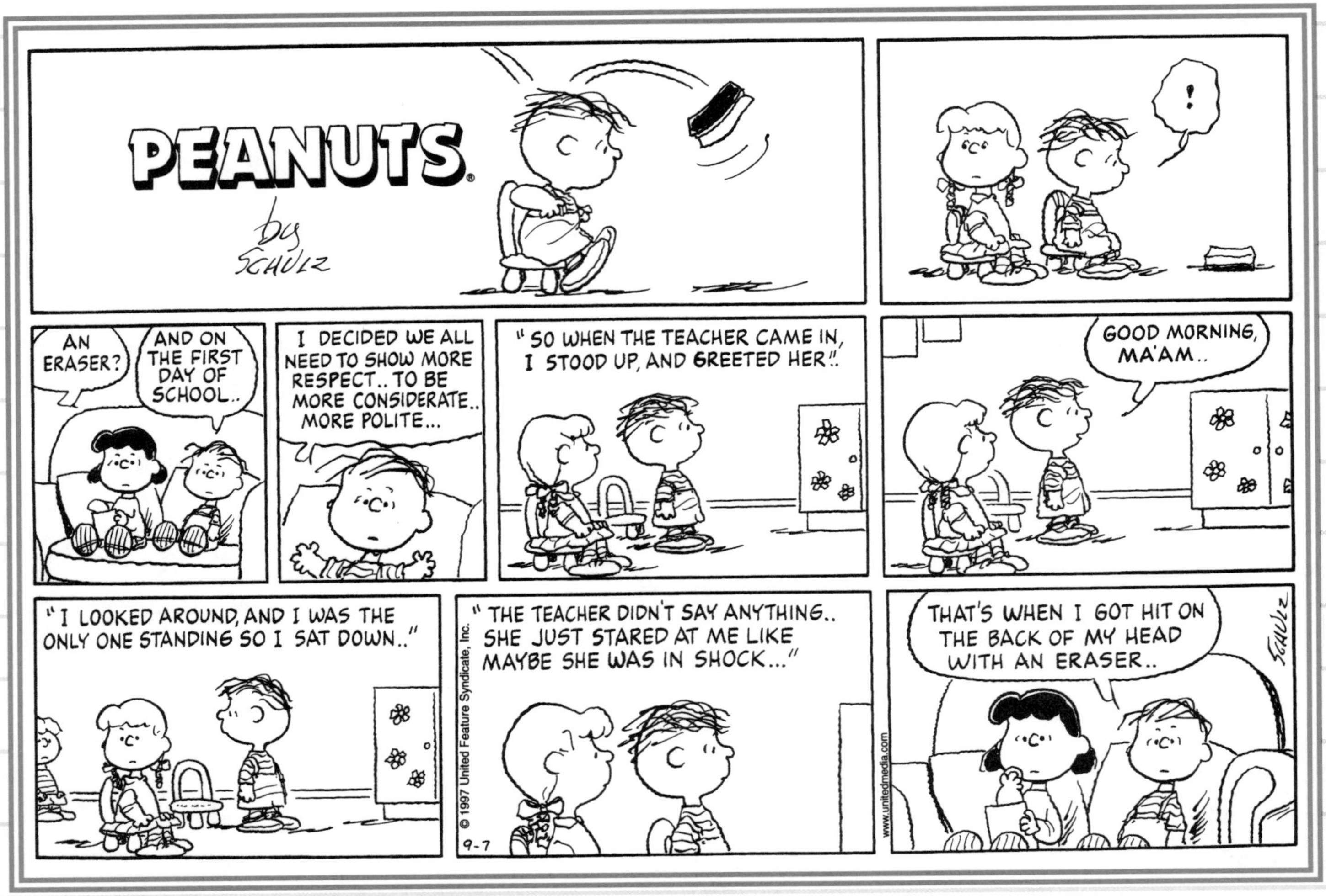
PEANUTS
by SCHULZ
!
AN ERASER?
AND ON THE FIRST DAY OF SCHOOL..
I DECIDED WE ALL NEED TO SHOW MORE RESPECT.. TO BE MORE CONSIDERATE.. MORE POLITE...
"SO WHEN THE TEACHER CAME IN, I STOOD UP, AND GREETED HER"!
GOOD MORNING, MA'AM..
"I LOOKED AROUND, AND I WAS THE ONLY ONE STANDING SO I SAT DOWN.."
"THE TEACHER DIDN'T SAY ANYTHING.. SHE JUST STARED AT ME LIKE MAYBE SHE WAS IN SHOCK..."
© 1997 United Feature Syndicate, Inc.
9-7
www.unitedmedia.com
THAT'S WHEN I GOT HIT ON THE BACK OF MY HEAD WITH AN ERASER..
SCHULZ

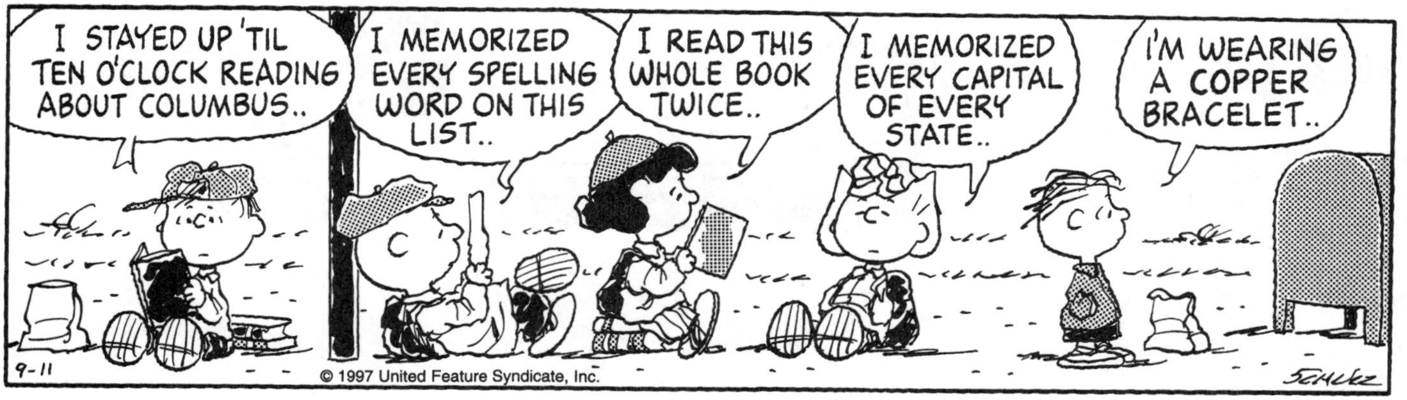
I STAYED UP 'TIL TEN O'CLOCK READING ABOUT COLUMBUS..
I MEMORIZED EVERY SPELLING WORD ON THIS LIST..
I READ THIS WHOLE BOOK TWICE..
I MEMORIZED EVERY CAPITAL OF EVERY STATE..
I'M WEARING A COPPER BRACELET..
9-11
© 1997 United Feature Syndicate, Inc.
SCHULZ

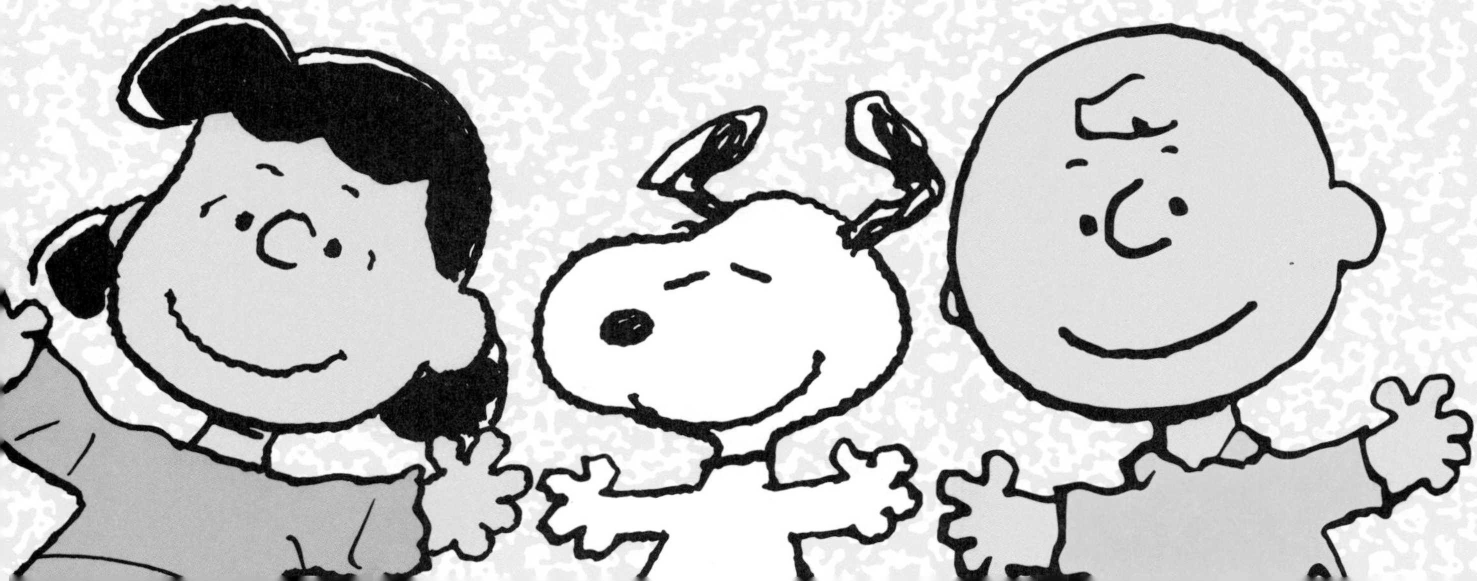

QUICK, MARCIE..I NEED A PENCIL AND SOME PAPER..
www.unitedmedia.com
AND I NEED AN ERASER, A PEN AND A RULER..
© 1997 United Feature Syndicate, Inc.
9-18
NO, MA'AM..I'M HER CADDIE..
SCHULZ

HEY, MARCIE..HOW SOON BEFORE SCHOOL STARTS AGAIN?
9-2
I MAY HAVE TO BORROW SOME NOTEBOOK PAPER AND THINGS..
www.snoopy.com
SO HOW SOON BEFORE SCHOOL STARTS?
DO YOU HAVE A CALENDAR?
© 1998 United Feature Syndicate, Inc.
A WHAT?
SCHULZ

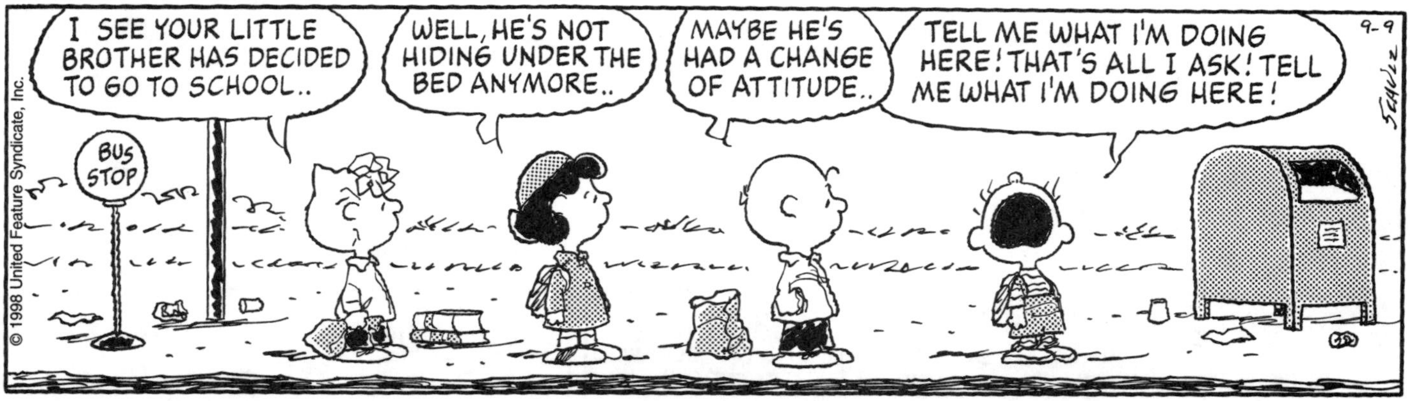
I SEE YOUR LITTLE BROTHER HAS DECIDED TO GO TO SCHOOL..
WELL, HE'S NOT HIDING UNDER THE BED ANYMORE..
MAYBE HE'S HAD A CHANGE OF ATTITUDE..
TELL ME WHAT I'M DOING HERE! THAT'S ALL I ASK! TELL ME WHAT I'M DOING HERE!
BUS STOP
9-9
SCHULZ
© 1998 United Feature Syndicate, Inc.

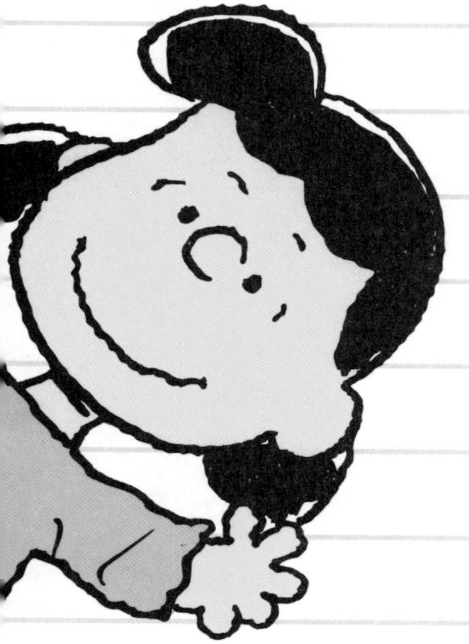